Waltharius

The Latin Epic of Walther of Aquitaine

WALTHARIUS

THE LATIN EPIC OF WALTHER OF AQUITAINE

Translated by
BRIAN MURDOCH

Edited by
LEONARD NEIDORF

UPPSALA BOOKS
London

UPPSALA BOOKS

London, England

www.uppsalabooks.com

Copyright © Uppsala Books 2025

ISBN 978-1-961361-21-8 Hardback

ISBN 978-1-961361-20-1 Paperback

All rights reserved.
Except for brief quotations used for purposes of review
or scholarly citation, no part of this publication may be
reproduced, stored in a retrieval system, or transmitted,
in any form or by any means, electronic, mechanical,
photocopying, recording, or otherwise,
without the prior permission of the publisher.

CONTENTS

Preface   i

Introduction   1

Bibliography   29

Waltharius: Text and Translation   48

Notes   141

Appendix: Two Latin Battle Poems   165

PREFACE

Waltharius, a Latin epic composed by a speaker of a Germanic language sometime in the ninth or tenth century, is one of the great monuments of medieval literature. As a complete and coherent work rooted in Germanic heroic legend, it deserves a readership comparable to other works fitting that description—e.g., *Beowulf*, the *Nibelungenlied*, the *Poetic Edda*, the *Saga of the Volsungs*—but it has never received such a readership. Whereas all of the aforementioned works are readily available in Penguin Classics and Oxford Classics volumes, *Waltharius* has never been included in any such series. The reason for this odd omission must be that *Waltharius* has been a treasure hoarded by professional scholars and narrow specialists. Insufficient efforts have been made to bring the poem to a wider audience, raise awareness of its value, and provide the reading public with an affordable and accessible book that equips readers with all they need to understand and appreciate this medieval masterpiece. The present book is intended to fix that.

The most recent English translation of *Waltharius*, that of Abram Ring (2016), is manifestly not intended to solve the aforementioned problem. Ring's introduction and notes constitute a valuable contribution to scholarship, but his translation cannot be recommended to readers wanting an unencumbered experience of the poem. A particularly rebarbative feature of his translation is its programmatic rendering of all Greek-derived vocabulary with French words, so that, for instance, Walther ludicrously says to Hildegund: "Do all these things cautiously and gradually *dans la semaine*." The French phrase is used in order to signal to the reader that the Greek loanword *ebdomada*, which is also found in the Vulgate, happens to appear in the text. Surely such information is not so vital that it should motivate the transformation of Walther into the pretentious sort of character who would pepper his speech with gratuitous French phrases. If that were not enough, the suggested retail price for Ring's translation ($63) confirms that its publisher intended it to be purchased primarily by university libraries.

Brian Murdoch first published a translation of *Waltharius* in 1989. His translation was extraordinary, in that it presented *Waltharius* as a literary work to be enjoyed rather than a coarse textual quarry to be mined for signs of Latin erudition or German barbarism. Of all existing translations, it is, in the view of the present editor, by far the most readable and compelling one available. The other English translations appear uninspired and pedantic in comparison. Unfortunately, Murdoch's translation was published by a small academic press with limited distribution. It fell out of print and became nearly impossible to obtain. The present book, featuring a revised and updated translation prepared by the translator in collaboration with the editor, is thus also intended to give Murdoch's rendition the readership it deserves.

Both the editor and the translator are indebted to more scholars than can be named in a short space. Leonard Neidorf thanks the members of his *Waltharius* reading group for their insightful comments and suggestions. He particularly wishes to thank Sam Lewis, Graham Scheper, Zixuan Wei, Na Xu, Yunshuo Zeng, and Chenyun Zhu for significant assistance provided during the preparation of this manuscript. Brian Murdoch records longstanding debts of gratitude to George Gillespie, Ute Schwab, Linda Archibald, Lewis Jillings, and Adrian Murdoch for providing him with published and unpublished material pertaining to *Waltharius*.

INTRODUCTION

J. R. R. Tolkien, in his seminal lecture on *"Beowulf*: The Monsters and Critics," summarizes the history of the poem's scholarship by relating, in rapid succession, the variety of conflicting opinions about *Beowulf* that have been confidently expressed by critics (1936: 249). If one were to attempt to do the same thing for *Waltharius*, it might read as follows:

> *Waltharius* was written in the early or late tenth century; it was written at the end or the middle of the ninth century; it was written in Carolingian times; it was written at the start of the eleventh century. It is anonymous; it is by Grimald of St Gallen; it is by Ekkehard I of St Gallen; it is by an unknown Frenchman; it is by an otherwise unknown monk called Gerald of St Gallen (of Strasbourg, of Toul, of Eichstätt, of somewhere else), who was German (French). It was written at St Gallen, Freising, Lorraine or somewhere else. Gerald's prologue is an integral author statement; it is quite separate and has nothing to do with the text. The prologue dedicates the work (the copy) to Bishop (or Archbishop) Erkambald of Strasbourg (of Eichstätt, of Mainz). It is in origin a Visigothic lay; it is an original work in Latin (though perhaps based on elements from known Germanic tales); it is a direct translation or adaptation of a German

epic. The Old English *Waldere* is earlier; *Waldere* is based upon *Waltharius*; these two works provide evidence of a Germanic Walther-saga; there is no Walther-saga.

A PROBLEMATIC WORK

Waltharius is an unusual text, and on acquaintance with its secondary literature, it becomes positively bewildering. It is Germanic insofar as it deals with Franks and Burgundians, and heroes with names like Gundahari or Walthari, and the latter's love, Hildigunda. Yet it is in Latin. The secondary literature quickly leaves the enquirer reeling, as study after study states with conviction that the work was composed anywhere between 800 and 1020, and is either anonymous, is by Ekkehard (Ekkehart) I, a monk from the famous monastery at St Gallen, or by a monk called Gerald, on whose origins no-one seems to agree. While other possible authors have also been put forward (Grimald of St Gallen is another), the three possibilities mentioned are those most frequently encountered. Not, of course, that Gerald is much of a help. Although three of the manuscripts—all of which date, incidentally, from the eleventh century or later, with one probable exception from the tenth century—carry a prologue in which a Geraldus seems to be claiming authorship, identifying him is not easy. He refers to a church dignitary, either a bishop or an archbishop, called Erkambald (Erchambold), but there are three candidates in question: either the Bishop of Eichstätt (882-911), or the Bishop of Strasbourg (965-991), or (the least likely of the candidates) the Archbishop of Mainz (1011-21).

All that can be agreed about the poem is that it is in Latin (although the implication is often there that it should not be, since it is really a Germanic epic), and that it is by a monk, who is casting what is clearly a Germanic theme into a would-be Vergilian mold, in hexameters, possibly as a kind of exercise or amusement in a monastic school. The author was assumed for a long time to be Ekkehard I of St Gallen, writing in about 930. This assumption was made by its first

INTRODUCTION

editor in 1838 and it held for about a century. The attribution is based on a reference in a history of St Gallen by Ekkehard IV in the eleventh century to a *Vita Waltharii manu fortis*, "Life of Walthari Stronghand," by his earlier namesake, who died in about 970. Some critics continue to favor this attribution (Langosch 1953, 1983; Zeydel 1959; Makkay 1998: 54; Ring 2016: 14), though it was brought into considerable doubt between the wars. Two things speak against it: the first, that there is no certainty that the work referred to by Ekkehard IV is the same as our poem; the second, the existence in two of the main manuscripts at least of the prologue by Gerald. Once the authorship of Ekkehard had been called into question, the date could be questioned, too. Wolf (1940-1 and 1954-5), followed by Strecker in his great edition (1951), proposed the early ninth century, still in the Carolingian age, but named no author. Later, Önnerfors (1979) suggested Grimald of St Gallen (d. 872), Werner (1990) suggested Ermoldus Nigellus (d. 838), and Dronke (1977) suggested that Theodulf (d. 821), the Visigothic Bishop of Orleans, might have transmitted to the court of Charlemagne the Visigothic lay upon which the poem is based. We are very much in the realms of speculation already, however, and arguments have been marshalled against these views (Schieffer 1980; Schaller 1983). Most recently, Stone (2013), Rio (2015), and Turcan-Verkerk (2016) champion ninth-century dates for *Waltharius*, finding the poem resonant with various aspects of ninth-century Frankish politics.

A body of scholarship accepts Gerald as the author, but once again opinions vary about him and who he was (the first editors saw him as *magister* in St Gallen correcting Ekkehard's work). Hauck (1954) placed him in the late ninth century, von den Steinen (1963) in the middle of that century, at the court of Lorraine. The suggestion that he was French has not been pursued far, and his language (even in the prologue only) shows him to have been German, since he plays on German words. He might, of course, have been writing in French territory: Bate (1978), arguing strongly for Gerald, suggests that he might have been at Toul. Many of the Gerald-group (Grégoire 1936; Stach 1943; Bate 1978) identify Erkambald as the Bishop of Strasbourg, although a case has been made for him as the rather earlier Bishop of Eichstätt (Hauck 1954). Erkambald, Archbishop of Mainz, is rather late, however, so that line has not really been pursued.

A scholarly poll on all this would probably result in equal honors for Gerald, Ekkehard, and Anonymous. There is, though, no firm connection between what Ekkehard IV says was written by his namesake and our poem, and the Gerald of the prologue is hard to dismiss. The argument that the styles of the prologue and the text differ sharply does not, of course, prove that the writers were different. To come down on the side of Gerald as the author, however, is no great step forward, since speculation once again comes into play about who he was or when he wrote. Clearly a pragmatic approach is necessary. The work is datable to the period 800-1000 (as outside limits), and the precise name of the author does not really matter in a period where so many works are anonymous (and which is being translated in an age where the concept of author has been, for many, deconstructed out of existence anyway). Two comments seem to sum up the problem. The entry for *Waltharius* in Henry and Mary Garland's *Oxford Companion to German Literature* (1976: 915) reads:

> The poem was formerly believed to be a school exercise done by Ekkehard I... of St Gall, who died in 973. This attribution is doubtful and recent scholarship inclines, though without certainty, to the view that the author was Geraldus, an otherwise unknown monk of the ninth century, probably of the time of Charlemagne...

The final 'probably' is, however, too strong. Secondly, Karl Strecker (1951: 2), although he argued for the early dating, nevertheless summarised in his last edition:

> Person des Dichters, Heimat des Gedichtes bleibt unbekannt, als sicher kann nur gelten, dass der Dichter ein Deutscher war... [The poet's identity and the poem's place of origin remain

INTRODUCTION

unknown, and the only thing that can be taken as certain is that the poet was German.]

Much of the secondary literature, as can be seen from these comments, has concerned itself with questions of authorship and date, neither of which need necessarily be very important. Yet recent scholarship continues to feature vigorous and productive discussion of these questions, taking them in new directions and finding new angles on the poem through historical contextualization (Stone 2013; Rio 2015; Turcan-Verkerk 2016; Ring 2016: 8-15). Beside the question of date and authorship, another enduring question is that of the origin of the work, which has been seen either as a Latin reflection of a Germanic Walther-saga, based on a German original, possibly coming from a Visigoth source (Dronke 1977); or, on the other hand, as an original in its own right (Panzer 1948), which in turn gave rise to other works, including the Old English *Waldere*. This question is discussed in more detail below.

One author, finally, who was sure of the authorship was Joseph Viktor von Scheffel, whose novel *Ekkehard* (1855) was enormously successful in the nineteenth and early twentieth century both in Germany and through translations in the Anglo-Saxon world and elsewhere, with numerous reprintings. Scheffel edited the text of *Waltharius* (most of which is in one of the final chapters of his novel) in 1874, and it remained in print for decades. His novel, however, gripped the imagination. A poem (ironically enough) based on it was published in 1879 by Countess Adèle Elise von Bredow-Goerre, and an opera by J. J. Abert in 1879, as well as a drama in English by E. S. Ross in the same year. None of these offshoots remain popular, but neither the novel nor the medieval Latin poem should be forgotten. *Waltharius* especially remains well worth reading, and one of the reasons for this is the reason given by Gerald in his prologue: for pure entertainment.

MANUSCRIPTS: FORM AND LANGUAGE

Waltharius is preserved in a healthy number of manuscripts. Four full versions survive, and there are eight fragmentary versions. Others, known to have existed once, are now lost. Strecker (1951) lists eighteen such manuscripts, although some of them might be identical with the fragments. The location of the manuscripts covers a broad area from northern France to southern Germany (Strecker distinguished between a northern and southern group), and the number of surviving manuscripts is a comparatively respectable one. The four full manuscripts are preserved in Brussels (originally from Gembloux, eleventh-century and designated B), in Paris (originally from Fleury or from Echternach, also eleventh-century and designated P), in Karlsruhe (from Hirsau, twelfth-century and designated K), and finally Trier (a late text, fifteenth-century, from Mettlach, designated T). The fragments range from a Hamburg manuscript dated by Bernhard Bischoff (although earlier writers placed it somewhat later) in the late tenth century, which seems therefore to confirm that the poem dates from before the year 1000, to copies made in the fifteenth century. Both B and P contain the prologue of Gerald, and Bate (1978: 2) refers to the quotation of a line from this prologue in 990, indicating that the text and the prologue were associated at an early stage. Some manuscripts (T, for example) do not have the author's postscript at the end. Ring's (2016: 20-4) introduction contains an excellent discussion of the manuscript evidence.

The meter of the poem is the Latin hexameter, that used by Vergil, consisting of six feet divided by the quantity of the sounds (long or short vowels determined either by nature or position), rather than by stress, as in modern English meters, even though speech-rhythms can play a part. The line consists of four dactyls or spondees, followed by an invariable dactyl and then a spondee (or a trochee). Using stresses instead of quantity, in fact, English-speaking schoolchildren learning to scan the *Aeneid* have tended to fix the typical ending of a hexameter in their minds by some mnemonic like "munching a/ beanstalk," "strawberry/ jam-pot" or something similar. Elisions of vowels sometimes occur, and a break in the line, a caesura, was flexible, but often came after the third foot. In the Middle Ages, a rhymed form developed (the so-called Leonine hexameter), and rhymes at the third foot (or even the second or fourth) occur in *Waltharius*, but the rhymes are usually on one syllable only—for example, on a single vowel in an ending, which often does not look like a rhyme to an English-speaker—or they are simply assonances, many of which would not really be felt to rhyme at all. It has been noted that there are relatively frequent alliterations in *Waltharius*, which is a feature of Germanic heroic verse, though it is also prominent in some of the Latin hexameter poems with which the poet was familiar.

The present translation is in an iambic verse, because runs of stress-based spondees or dactyls in modern English are hard to make effective. As an example of the original meter, however, a famous line towards the end may serve:

sic sic armillas partiti sunt Avarenses (1404)

The line is scanned:

// // // ///--//

The rhythm might be imitated in English stressed verse by something like:

Thus, thus, some Hun gold rings now were given to each man

As an example of a rhyme on a single final syllable, the following line from the early part of the poem contains the feature:

Quorum rex Gibich<u>o</u> solio polleat in alt<u>o</u> (14)

For an example of assonance, see the following line:

Hoc melius fore quam vit*am* simul ac region*em* (25)

There is a sequence of alliteration in the following passage, as well as single-syllable rhyme and assonance:

In castrum venit atque pedes stetit ante puellae
Ipsa metu perculsa sonum prompsit muliebrem.
At postquam tenuis redit in praecordia sanguis,
Paulum suspiciens spectat, num viveret heros. (891-4)

A few other features of the language may be noted. Quotations from Vergil abound, and there are many from other writers too, including Lucan, Statius, and Prudentius. Strecker's 1951 edition lists correspondences in the notes, although they are at times not entirely convincing, or at least not very useful. That the poet borrows a great amount from the *Aeneid*, however, is undeniable. Features of the *Aeneid*, too, are imitated as when, for example, the poet marks the passing of time by referring to Phoebus, or Hesperos, or indulges in an extended image (sometimes self-consciously). The clear humor in the work, though, is not matched in the *Aeneid*. Overall, the fact that the writer is constructing his poem in a style consciously imitative of the structure of the *Aeneid* has frequently been pointed out, as has, indeed, the dominant role of Vergil's poem throughout the Middle Ages. It is not an accident that this is a piece by a young man, perhaps a scholarly exercise, albeit one that was brilliantly executed. The *Aeneid* has been a set book in schools of all sorts virtually since it was saved from destruction on Vergil's death at the insistence of Augustus.

Nevertheless, this Latin is not the same as Vergil's, and the meter too cannot be treated as if it were Vergil—we are in a later stage of verse and the whole question of rhyme is a new development, for example. The poet also indulges in wordplay (Ziolkowski 2001), not only within Latin but also between Latin and German (the best-known being that on Hagano's name and the word for a hawthorn). In the language too, problems arise, not only with unclassical words or

INTRODUCTION

variations (many noted by Strecker 1951 and Bate 1978), but with unusual utterances, the most celebrated being the quite un-Vergilian *Wah! sed quid dicis...* (l. 1429). Names, of course, cause prosodic problems, and although some are unproblematic, such as Attila, and some can be Latinized comfortably, such as Guntharius (although he appears once in a Germanic form as Gunthere) others are more complex—Hiltgunt (her name varies in different manuscripts) being a prime example, even if in this form she fits well into a hexameter spondee, as does Helmnot.

Gerald's prefatory piece or prologue, finally, is rather different, and some critics have used the fact that the two styles are dissimilar to argue against his authorship. The rhymes are much clearer, and there are again wordplays between German and Latin (on the name Erkambald, for example). Nevertheless, there is no reason to suppose that a single writer could not use two different styles for two different purposes, so that the difference in styles is not much of an argument for different authorship.

HISTORICAL ECHOES

One of the features of the heroic epic is that it typically bears a loose relationship to identifiable historical events or characters. These events may be contemporary, but interpreted in a heroic manner, such as the death of Byrhtnoth in the Old English poem *The Battle of Maldon*. A more usual state of affairs is for them to reflect the history of a far earlier period. This can apply to primary or secondary epic (though *Waltharius* again confuses things by being what looks like a primary epic in the clothing of a secondary epic); the historical basis of the *Nibelungenlied* is as remote from Middle High German as the fall of Troy was from Vergil. This means that the historical events and characters upon which the story is (loosely) founded are changed, distorted, and sometimes given entirely new roles. In historical terms, heroic epics need preserve no more than a memory of isolated events from a far earlier time, and the attempt to combine historical and literary judgements is full of dangers for both disciplines. Most of the Germanic poems (even one as unusual as *Waltharius*) present recognizable figures in roles that are not the same as those they have in contemporary non-literary sources. We must be prepared for very considerable distortions of history and sometimes geography.

How much does all this matter? We may read the *Nibelungenlied* as the story of a dominant woman (Kriemhilt) and her increasingly single-minded desire for revenge and for the power that a treasure which was once hers can represent. But behind it is still a memory of the defeat of the Burgundian Gundahari at the hands of the Huns, and also of the separate fact that Attila, the great leader of the Huns, stands in effect at the end of Hunnish hegemony, and that he died just after his marriage to a Germanic princess. The heroic epic can often retain essentials, and can afford us a glimpse that is more vivid than we have in the somewhat bare chronicles, of the world of the Germanic tribes— Burgundians, Goths, Vandals, Lombards, Franks—in the fourth, fifth and sixth centuries, and that of their great adversaries, the Romans in Gaul or Byzantium, and the Huns, Avars, and Slavs in the east. The memory of these earlier battles may also overlap with (and gain relevance for) more contemporary events, and may be adapted to fit them: Vikings interchange with Saracens; Huns, Avars and Magyars all merge. In *Waltharius* nearly all the major figures may be linked with historical persons, but not to the same extent. Further, the poet has, as it were, the right people in the right places, but he makes them members of the groups who occupied those places in his own time, not in the time at which the originals lived.

The best-known identifiable figure is probably Attila the Hun, ruler of a large area, who made major attacks on the declining Roman empire in the east and the west, though he was defeated by a Roman army under Aetius, aided by the Visigoths, Franks, Burgundians, Saxons and others in an important battle in Gaul in 451. He died in 453 on his wedding night to a Germanic princess called Hildico (Chaucer tells us in *The Pardoner's Tale*, ll. 579-82, that he was drunk at the time, an interesting tradition in the light of our poem), and his empire went thereafter into a decline. His center, in the Roman province of Pannonia, was later occupied by the Avars and then by the Magyars. That Attila, who is presented in such a strong light at the opening of the work, should fade out of the story after the escape of the last of his hostages is almost a reflection of his own fate and that of his empire, although the fear of the later Avars remains. The historical name of his queen in *Waltharius* is not identifiable, however. He appears to have had numerous wives or concubines, of which the names of only two, Kerka and (H)ildico, survive in historical sources.

If Attila is an historical figure with a roughly correct role in the right place, the Guntharius of the poem comes close. He can be identified with Gundahari (Gundicarius in Latin sources), king of the Burgundians, who ruled at Worms and who would presumably have claimed descent from the Gibica named as one of the ancient kings in the Laws of the Burgundians, and who has given his name to the father in *Waltharius*. He was a rough contemporary only of Attila. In 436 Gundahari and the Burgundians appear to have been defeated by the Huns acting as mercenaries for the Romans, and they moved then to southern Gaul, to present day Burgundy. They assisted the Romans against Attila himself in 451, and so we have a parallel of the defeat of the Burgundians and the later rejection of the pact with the Huns. Even historical sources mix up the two events, and have Attila fighting directly against Gundahari (Learned 1892: 164). Learned also points out that a Greek source refers to a figure probably identifiable with Gundahari, who joined with Goar, ruler of the Alans, another tribe, who might be a prototype for Hagano, and he notes further that this figure in literature might also have taken on elements from Gundericus, king of the Vandals at the beginning of the fourth century.

At all events, Gundahari, who appears in a number of Germanic poems, most notably as Gunther in the *Nibelungenlied* and Gunnarr in *Atlakviða*, is preserved as a man who is defeated. The memory of the fall of the Burgundians is strong. However, the poet of *Waltharius* makes Gundahari into a Frank, the group which occupied at the time of the poem the place left by the Burgundians on the Rhine and at

Worms, and ascribes to the Burgundians the essentially fictitious characters Hildigunda and her father Heririk. The former name might have links with (H)ildico and a character with the latter's name (Hereric) is mentioned in *Beowulf* (l. 2206), but not much can be said about their potential historicity. Both Attila and Gundahari move from history to literature with a certain ambiguity. The former was clearly a powerful ruler, but he fades from sight, just as the great leader of the Huns was indeed defeated. Gundahari is remembered in association with the fall of the Burgundians, but also in the context of the Burgundian assistance at the defeat of Attila.

Gundahari, then, is made into a Frank, and he has beside him his vassal Hagano, who plays in many others works (e.g., the *Nibelungenlied*) a similar role to that in *Waltharius*, of the subordinate stronger than the king himself. He is, if the concept is possible, more fictional than his master. He may perhaps be identified with an historical figure referred to briefly above—that is, with Goar, ruler (or *khagan*—whence perhaps the name, which then overlaps with the German for a hawthorn) of the Alans, an originally nomadic group who moved across Europe and merged eventually with the Vandals in Spain. Various other possibilities have been put forward for a prototype for Hagano, including the Roman prefect Aetius (also suggested as the model for Hagano's father) and a duke Aigyna who fought for the Franks and Burgundians in the seventh century. All three possibilities allow for an association with Gundahari, of course (or with the Burgundians at least). Much has been written on his localisation in the *Nibelungenlied* as Hagen of Tronje, and the place has been variously identified from Belgium to Alsace. There is a certain symbolic value in his linking in *Waltharius* with Troy, however. Of all the characters, he has the most literary role—the man torn by loyalty to king or friend—and he has many of the best speeches. Whatever his origins, it is clear that he is a vehicle for characterisation, rather than for the reflection of actual events. Attempts have been made to identify the various opponents of Walthari (Learned 1892: 175), but none is convincing and, more to the point, none adds much to the appreciation of the poem. Walthari himself, however, is the son of King Alphari of Aquitaine. Various instances of a Waltharius in Lombardic writings are known, as also is a Frankish duke Walaric, but it is noteworthy that here the poet uses a regional rather than national designation. At the time of the poem, this region was in West Frankish hands, having fallen to the Merovingian Franks in 507. But at the time of Gundahari and Attila, Aquitaine was a Visigothic kingdom, and the identification of Waltharius with Wal(l)ja, a Visigothic king at Toulouse at the beginning of the fifth century (Grégoire 1936: 212; Münkler 1983: 46-56) is probably correct. In this case, though, only the name, the general bravery in battle against other Germanic tribes, and the Visigoth role against the Huns in 451 seem relevant. For our poem, the far more important association with Hildigunda and the conflict of loyalty with Hagano situate Walthari on the side of the literary rather than the historical figures.

LITERARY ANALOGUES—AND A SAGA?

There are several literary analogues to *Waltharius*, if that is the appropriate term for texts whose relationship may either be very close indeed (Strecker 1951 includes the Latin prose of the *Chronicon Novaliciense* in his list of manuscripts) or it may consist of nothing more than shared names (e.g., Walther and Hildegund) or a Walther character from somewhere that might be linked with Aquitaine, the Huns, or the Vosges. In fact, one striking thing about the analogues is how different they are from our text in many respects (see Learned 1892: 131-54 for a schematic overview of the poem's narrative incidents and their presence or absence in the analogues; see also the excellent comparative analysis in Bornholdt 2005: 42-85). Many analogues, however, do contain the essential elements of a warrior named Walther and a lady named Hildegund in flight from a place where they have been hostages or exiles, a pursuit and combat of some kind, and a return home in triumph.

There is debate on whether the Old English fragmentary epic of *Waldere* (Schwab 1967; Zettersten 1979; Himes 2009; Shippey &

Neidorf 2024: 361-77) or our poem has chronological precedence, and many scholars have taken the existence of the Old English poem as evidence of an ancient Germanic Walther-poem or a Walther-saga. The fragments are, however, very brief, and the relative chronology is far from clear if *Waltharius* is not the tenth-century poem composed by Ekkehard that it was once believed to be. If there is no direct connection between the two works, the existence of *Waldere* might indicate that there was a known story of a fight involving Waldere (son of Ælfhere, champion of Attila), Hagen and Guðhere. As far as it is possible to tell, the relationship of content seems close. The two fragments show first someone, probably Hildeguð, encouraging Waldere to fight, and secondly another speaker referring to the history of a sword, followed by a challenge to Guðhere from Waldere. By all appearances, the poem featured the escape of Waldere and Hildeguð from the Hunnish court with treasure, the pursuit by Guðhere, and the ambivalence of Hagen.

Waldere and *Waltharius* are the oldest texts. Next comes the Latin prose version of parts of what is effectively *Waltharius* found in some of the chapters of a chronicle written in Novale, in Piedmont, not far from Turin, in the early eleventh century. The *Chronicon Novaliciense* (Learned 1892: 44-61; Magoun & Smyser 1950: 38-40; Schwab 1967: 273-9), some of which is about a different person also named Waltharius, has most of the story, but significantly not the ending.

The Middle High German *Nibelungenlied* at the beginning of the thirteenth century has brief references to the story in three strophes (nos. 1756, 1797, and 2344; see Learned 1892: 64; Edwards 2010), but displays in spite of the brevity a clear knowledge of its outline. Roughly contemporary, the poet Walther von der Vogelweide has a reference to the names of Walther and Hildegund (with a play with his own) in a lyric, while much later the poem *Von dem übelen wibe* also has a reference to the two names in conjunction (Learned 1892: 62 ff. and 123). Furthermore, there are in Middle High German a number of fragments and references in other texts from the thirteenth century or later that bear witness to a story involving Walther and Hildegund.

INTRODUCTION

Most important are two fragments, one in Graz and the other in Vienna (Learned 1892: 65-72; Magoun & Smyser 1950: 42-7; Schwab 1967: 279-89), the first referring to the earlier betrothal of the two lovers, the second to their return to Walther's homeland. Both are brief and develop the legendary matter in a far courtlier manner than *Waltharius* does. Beside the independent survivals, evidence of knowledge of a warrior called Walther with some of the past history of our central figure is found in references in the so-called *Dietrich-Epics*. Walther appears in *Biterolf und Dietleib*, *Alpharts Tod*, the *Rosengarten*, *Dietrichs Flucht* and the *Rabenschlacht* (most of the relevant extracts are in Learned 1892: 73-92; see Norman 1933: 10 ff. for a summary of the image of Walther in Middle High German sources). Further north, too, the Old Norse *Þiðreks saga*, also of the thirteenth century and with versions in Old Swedish (Learned 1892: 93-104; Magoun & Smyser 1950: 48-50; Schwab 1967: 271-3), seems related to the Middle High German versions. There is, at present, no book that compiles all of the medieval German references to the Walther legend and provides modern English translations of these texts; many of the relevant passages have never been translated into English. The present editor and translator are currently collaborating on a book intended to remedy this problem (*The Legend of Walther of Aquitaine: Medieval German Texts and Translations*), which is expected to be published by Uppsala Books in 2025.

The story is quite widespread. In Poland, the Latin *Chronicon Poloniae*, *Wielkopolska Kronika* of Boguphalus II, who died in 1253, contains the story of a Polish *Walterus robustus* (who is given the Polish name *wdaly Walczerz*) and his French wife Helgunda; there is an escape episode, but otherwise few similarities, and it ends with the adultery of Helgunda, who is then killed with her lover by Walterus (Learned 1892: 104-9; Magoun & Smyser 1950: 51-62; Schwab 1967: 290 ff.). Later versions in the Polish language also exist (Learned 1892: 110-22) from the sixteenth to the nineteenth century.

Walthari alone appears to have an independent existence as a warrior in the Old French *Chanson de Roland*, where he is called

Gualt(i)er(s) del Hum (perhaps 'from the land of the Huns') in the eleventh or early twelfth century, and he is there too in a Middle High German adaptation, Konrad the priest's *Rolandslied*, where he is simply called Walthere (Learned 1892: 124-9; Millet 1995; Beckmann 2010: 5-52). It is possible that *Waltharius* had a direct influence on other aspects of the *Chanson de Roland*, however (Tavernier 1914). Last of all, the figures of Walther and Hildegund may filter into Romance (Spanish, Catalan) ballads, the hero perhaps appearing as Gaiferos, and he and his lover are hostages escaping from the Moors (Dronke 1977; Ziolkowski 2012).

Even if it is unclear whether there was a saga, or a Germanic source for *Waltharius*, *Waltharius* can be read perfectly well without reference to any other work, and it is possible that it stands at the beginning, with all the analogues deriving from it. But it is rather difficult to fit the Old English *Waldere* into such a scheme. Even with the other analogues, though, there may not be enough there really to constitute a saga. At all events, the poet of *Waltharius* did not create his characters, and it is likely that he knew of them in a context. It is also likely that the contexts were stories, perhaps concerning a betrothal of two hostages (and their flight), and a battle between three men, one of them torn between friendship and loyalty as a vassal. It remains unclear whether or not these stories were in the form of songs, to what extent they were combined, what else they contained (the poet refers to one of Walthari's adversaries as if his name were from some source in line 688), or whether or not *Waldere* represents such a tradition. Any possible Germanic original adapted or translated by the poet would, though, have been very different from the *Waltharius* we have. The Vergilian structure and some of the attitudes are from a monastic mind, and it is hard to conceive of a Germanic epic poem ending with the joking indulged in by the two main characters. Not, of course, that all Germanic heroic poems end tragically, though many do. *Kudrun*, for example, ends in diplomatic harmony, even though a lot of blood has been shed on the way. If the events in *Waltharius* seem to be leading to tragedy, then the ending looks like an avoidance. It has been

INTRODUCTION

pointed out that although the central characters appear elsewhere in Germanic poetry, nowhere do they have the distinctive wounds sustained at the end of our poem. It is probably incorrect to think of a fixed Walther-saga, and better to think of narrative elements attached to historical or legendary Germanic figures that were adapted very greatly by individual medieval authors, including the poet of *Waltharius*.

The poem belongs, of course, to no genre: it is a one-off. It is not quite a Germanic heroic poem, although it has very many features in common with such poems, apart from its language. It has clearly been Christianized—Walthari's insistent chastity is an obvious example—but it is expressly not a work of piety. Nor, however, is it really a Vergilian epic; it has too many elements of humor for that. It has, of course, been argued that the whole work is a kind of joke at the expense of the Germanic epic (Parkes 1974; Kratz 1980), but although the poet's sense of humor cannot be denied (it is self-ironic, even at the expense of his own style at times), there is plenty of seriousness there too. The central character fights a whole series of battles for his life, love, and property, and the themes are serious enough. Only the ending turns away from tragedy. It might be thought of as "light entertainment" with no clear moral purpose (Ghosh 2013: 178-83), though many such purposes have been and continue to be discerned in the work. Nor, finally, is this a straightforward romance, for all that the lovers declare themselves, run away together, and eventually live happily ever after. *Waltharius* combines elements from many genres, and this is one of the reasons it is worth reading. At the same time, it can provoke thoughts about the nature of any of those genres, perhaps most especially the Germanic heroic epic, to which it may be an affectionate response.

WALTHARIUS *AND GERMANIC HEROIC POETRY*

Heroic poetry is, of course, concerned largely with bravery in battle, but this is not necessarily the essential theme, at least not of the

Germanic heroic epic. Different themes underpin the motif of the undaunted warrior. The first is personal: the warrior is concerned with fame, or more specifically with not being regarded in a bad light. Sigurd in one of the Eddic poems (*Grípisspá*) has his future life put before him by a soothsayer, but is concerned mainly to know whether after his life (which is clearly going to be of tragic complexity) any mocking songs will be sung about him; another Eddic poem (*Hávamál* st. 77) stresses that although cattle and kinsmen die, the reputation of the warrior does not (Murdoch 1996: 16-22). It is reputation, too, that forces Hildebrand to fight his son in the Old High German *Hildebrandslied* (Shippey & Neidorf 2024: 378-83). He is being watched by two armies: if he were to refuse to fight after his abortive attempt at rapprochement, the song composed about the battle afterwards would not be the tragic-elegiac *Hildebrandslied*.

But the themes of the Germanic heroic epic go beyond personal considerations. One of the most significant issues is far simpler: it is gold, not necessarily for its own sake, but for the power that gold represents. Even on the personal level, much of the *Hildebrandslied* hinges upon the possession of the armor and accoutrements of the older man. The *Nibelungenlied* has at its center the treasure of the Nibelungen, and on it rested a portion of Siegfried's prestige. On his death, Hagen has to remove it to prevent Siegfried's widow from purchasing soldiers, and at the very end it is the treasure that Kriemhild demands back. So too the gold rings, the *armillas*, stand at the center of *Waltharius*, representing the tribute money paid to the Huns, and the treasure that has to be divided amongst the same groups after the effective collapse of Hun resistance. Those *armillas* are the spoils of the fallen empire of Attila.

This does not mean that pugnaciousness and greed are the overriding forces of Germanic heroic poetry, of course. A further, and larger-scale theme of the Germanic epic is political, and the concern is for a balance of power and stability (Murdoch 1996). Power—and military power in particular that can be purchased with gold—is needed by a state for its survival. Sometimes a state which is under

INTRODUCTION

threat from some outside force must buy or entice outside assistance—as Beowulf is brought in to aid against the outside threat represented by Grendel. Sometimes, a bid for power does not work. In *Vǫlundarkviða*, an Eddic poem whose theme is of very considerable antiquity, the metal-worker Wayland the Smith, who can work gold but also weapons, the master technician, is kidnapped to work for a king on whom he takes a terrible revenge, killing his sons and impregnating his daughter to ensure that his child, the sole surviving grandchild of the king, will inherit, before he uses his technical skills to escape. The *Nibelungenlied*, too, is essentially a documentation of political failure, as the slighted sister seeks revenge for her murdered husband (killed in an attempt to maintain stability within the kingdom) by an outside alliance. On the other hand, a work like *Kudrun* offers a blueprint for government in a heroic age, as alliances are struck and sealed through marriage, once the would-be ally has proved his worth, and patience of many years has had to be exercised before one of the unworthy can be overcome. All these works, though rooted in Germanic history far earlier than the works themselves, clearly had a relevance (and more particularly a warning) for their own times, and perhaps have not entirely lost it. Industrial poaching and disastrous alliances are not restricted to the bronze age.

The themes of reputation (the cumulation of heroic attributes of bravery, single-mindedness and loyalty to friends, country, or cause, in the face of an enemy who could be a monster or a friend or relative) and of political stability go together, too. Beowulf himself rules for fifty years in peace, though the focus of the work is on his exploits as an individual. *Kudrun* shows the build-up of a network of alliances assisted by the strong arm of the unflinchingly loyal warrior Wate. It is easy to overlook, too, the fact that Walthari—whom we see for the most part as a warrior in his youth, when he is being tested—rules well for thirty years.

Waltharius has many of the attributes of a Germanic heroic epic—Smyser & Magoun (1941: 111) refer to it quite specifically as "this most important West Germanic heroic poem" in spite of its language.

The context is that of the Germanic past, and the themes of reputation and bravery are clear. Walthari himself is a resourceful warrior who stands his ground and fights to defend himself against great odds. Perhaps more significant, however, is Hagano, his friend. It is of interest that the *explicit* of the Brussels manuscript refers to the work as 'a book about the two friends Walthari and Hagano' (on the theme of friendship, see Flatt 2016). Walthari has no real option but to fight—he is trapped. His chief attribute is being able to fight exceptionally well. Hagano, however, is interesting because he does not want to fight at all, torn as he is between loyalty to his old friend and his loyalty as a vassal to king Gundahari, a loyalty that remains forceful despite the king's weakness and viciousness. Hagano is described as a vassal quite specifically, just as Gundahari attracts the attributive 'crazy' (*demens*) on several occasions. It is loyalty to his king that wins in Hagano, although this is only after he has seen that Gundahari is himself more concerned about reputation than loss of men—that he is behaving, in effect, as a hero should. Walthari cannot believe Hagano's betrayal of their friendship, of course, but nevertheless must fight his friend to save his own life and reputation. For him to fail to do so would mean the surrender of all the Hunnish gold and indeed of Hildigunda. It should not be forgotten that there are during the fighting scenes various attempts at negotiation on Walthari's part, none of which is accepted.

Other elements in the tale are less in line with the Germanic epic, apart from its Latinity. Hildigunda is betrothed to Walthari, and he treats her with a somewhat exaggeratedly chaste respect that is not commonly found in Germanic epic. She is not as prominent as she might be in a conventional romance; indeed, her subordinate ranking to the treasure-chests and the horse in the demand made of Walthari when he is first challenged may not depend only on the exigencies of meter. Her presence is nevertheless at least a nod towards the genre of romance. If Walthari's chastity is a Christian virtue, however, the poem is not Christian *rather than* Germanic. Certainly, Walthari prays before battle and makes the nice distinction between the sin and the sinner,

INTRODUCTION

hoping piously to meet in heaven those he has just somewhat extravagantly beheaded (indeed, his preoccupation with severed heads is one of the most curious features of the work). But this is merely an interlude. Roland, too, in the French *Chanson* at least (Konrad's German adaptation is a little different) confesses his general sins in a *mea culpa* before the final battle, but the fact that he has just committed the rearguard to fight against overwhelming odds in an act of heroic bravado and the desire, once again, that people shall not sing the wrong kind of songs about him are probably not among the sins he has in mind. God occasionally intervenes in the heroic epic, too, as when Wate's effective hijacking of the pilgrim ships in *Kudrun* carries them to disaster, explicitly because God avenges his own, and matters are not resolved until Queen Hilde has built and endowed a cathedral in expiation, something in which Wate ostensibly takes very little interest.

The effect of Christianity is probably seen most clearly at the end of the work. If we were dealing with a Germanic heroic poem, pure and simple, everything in the final parts, the fight of Walthari against the Franks, seems to be leading to a tragic outcome. We should perhaps expect that Gundahari would fall, and that Walthari would face Hagano alone in a battle which would have provided Hagano with his severest test, loyalty to the dead king or to his friend. And in that battle—although we must be aware that speculation is never very satisfactory—Walthari might well have fallen, a faint echo of the fact that the Visigoths did in fact fall to the Franks.

But this is, of course, precisely not how the work ends, for all that the ending we have looks like a compromise (Harms 1963: 111). It looks like the avoidance of a tragic outcome, although this does not mean, incidentally, that the poet is working from a Germanic source that ended tragically. He might as easily have composed up to that point in Latin a poem in the mold of the Germanic heroic epic, but wished at the end to avoid a tragedy that was looking so inevitable. It is entirely possible, moreover, that the poet was working within a tradition about Walther that already featured a happy ending, in which none of the principal characters was killed. Perhaps the strongest consideration in support of that hypothesis is that there is no hint of a tragic ending in any of the extant sources and analogues (a point made cogently by Dronke 1977: 31-2). Of all the references to Walther in Old English, Old Norse, Middle High German, and Polish, there is not one that records or implies a tragic outcome to his tale. Furthermore, Claudia Bornholdt (2005: 42-85) argues persuasively for a connection between the Walther tradition and Germanic bridal-quest narratives, which typically feature a happy ending. If Bornholdt is correct, then it is all the more likely that the poet's hypothetical source did not end tragically, and ended rather with the homecoming and marriage of Walther and Hildegund.

It is significant that the details of the ending are unique. Walthari and the others are known elsewhere, but not as one-handed, one-eyed or one-legged. Bate (1978: 66-7) points out the link between these injuries and the biblical passages advocating the removal of the right eye or right hand or of an unspecified leg if they should offend. For all that, the poet's next thought is that this is how the gold of the Huns was shared—between the Germanic tribes, but only after bloodshed. And in spite of the joking session between Hagano and Walthari, the wounds are bound up, and Walthari returns to rule, with his share, we presume, of the Hun spoils.

Whether or not the poet is following a specific source or whether he is constructing a story of his own, he does it with some success. Much critical energy has been expended upon questions that will probably never be solved, but critics have also affirmed the value of a work which has many features of the Germanic heroic epic, but which in its avoidance of a final tragedy throws light on the genre as a whole. Three comments are worth repeating. Discussing the Germanic background, Paul Klopsch (1963: 59) writes:

> Trotz der Versetzung des germanischen Stoffes in eine christliche Welt und in ihre lateinische Weltsprache [ist *Waltharius*] eine künstlerische Einheit.

INTRODUCTION

[In spite of the transference of Germanic material into a Christian world and into Latin, its universal language, *Waltharius* remains an artistic unity.]

Walther Haug (1984: 11) makes clear the relationship with the heroic epic, referring to the poem as:

> eine strategisch raffinierte kritische Umdeutung der Heldensage.
> [a strategically sophisticated critical transformation of the heroic saga.]

Max Wehrli (1965: 72-3), finally, summarises the combination of elements in the work:

> Es bleibt der Zauber des *Waltharius*, wie hier zwischen germanischen, antiken und christlichen Möglichkeiten versucht ist, einen neuen, selbständigen Weg zu finden, ironisch oft, spielerisch und widerspruchsvoll, aber doch und vor allem mit der Neugier und Frische eines folgenreichen Beginns.
> [The magic of *Waltharius* remains in its attempt to find a new and independent way through Germanic, classical, and Christian possibilities, often ironic, playful, and contradictory, but still, and above all with the curiosity and freshness of a fruitful beginning.]

Amongst those who have praised the poem for its own sake, R. R. Bolgar (1954: 192 ff.) indicates the amount of influence it had on later works.

The tale of Walthari, the Visigoth of Aquitaine, has its roots amongst the Germanic tribes of the fifth century in conflict with the Huns and with each other. We can identify Attila, and also Gundahari, but we are less sure of an historical basis for Hagano, in many ways the most memorable of the limited cast of characters, whose heroic loyalty is actually put to the test, not just his courage, which goes without saying for most heroes. The central figure, Walthari, though perhaps based on a Visigothic king just as remote as Hagano's suggested original, is effectively a literary figure. Although he fights alone in some literary works, he is usually linked with his lover, Hildigunda. History and epic and a little romance are linked, and at risk of stretching a metaphor beyond its proper limits, the final combat, between Walthari and Hagano after the wounding of Gundahari (and long after Attila has bowed out of the tale) places in the foreground a fight of the tragic Germanic heroic epic against the novelty of romance, whilst history looks on in confusion, until the Church steps in and stops the fight.

THE TRANSLATION

Two possibilities present themselves in translating a poetic work: the form can be imitated, or the work can be put into prose. Sometimes the latter is advisable: the *Nibelungenlied*, for example, has a verse form which is unusual to a modern ear, and even rhymed couplets can very easily fail. Making rhyme plausible across the languages and years is the most difficult of tasks. The decision to translate into verse is somewhat easier if a free-verse form may justifiably be used. The pseudo-Vergilian *Waltharius*, if translated into prose, reads very flatly, however, rather like a crib of Caesar. Accordingly, translating the poem into a fairly free iambic unrhymed verse, predominantly hexameters, seems a reasonable compromise. Actual imitation of Vergilian hexameters, matching stress for quantity, is very difficult indeed, and with *Waltharius* it would be impossible to imitate the rhymes and assonances, the alliterations and the wordplays, although an attempt has been made with Gerald's metrically rather different prologue. In general terms, an ideal model might be, perhaps, the C. Day Lewis translation of Vergil, which avoids any rhythmic persistence. In (necessary) default of that, something like Alfred Noyes' *Drake*, in form if not in substance, might do, though not, perhaps Katherine Buck's over-

INTRODUCTION

archaising *Wayland-Dietrich* Saga of the 1920s. Against the charge that the present offering is hardly up to the standard of Day Lewis, it might be said that the poem itself is not Vergil, even if whole lines are sometimes lifted from the *Aeneid*. At all events, the aim has been to put *Waltharius* into a readable modern poetic form, to make it accessible to those interested in medieval poetry.

Translating a medieval work—by which is meant, making it engaging and comprehensible to a modern reader—demands some modifications of the text. One such is in the rendering of the names. They are of course Latinized in the original, but Waltharius remains in spite of its ending clearly an un-classical name, and so does Hagano, for example. Some of the names are less than familiar in any language, and have to be left alone, like Kamalo or Kimo. Walter, on the other hand, only has connotations in English of a faintly old-fashioned nature, and at the other extreme it would be hard to find an equivalent for Gibicho, so we have given the characters' names in their oldest, and hence most foreign-looking versions, to remind us that the roots of the tale are in the formative years of Europe. Attila, who declines quite well in his pre-Sound Shift form, is familiar enough anyway. We have also used "Hun" for any description of his people, even though the Latin also uses *Avares*, the Avars, as well as variations on Pannonia. One liberty we have taken is to give Attila's queen the name Ospirina, partly to give her a feminine ending, but also, be it admitted, to move her further away from a proprietary painkiller. She matches none of Attila's known queens in any case, and so the liberty is probably pardonable. For similar reasons, in the two poems translated as an appendix, Charlemagne's son's honorable Merovingian name (Pippin) is given the French form Pepin: for better or worse, Pippin connotes either an apple or a character in Tolkien. The translator always has to be on the lookout for the unconsciously ridiculous in the target language: the word *nodosus*, "knotty," applied to an ash-wood spear can all too easily come to sound like a celebrated suburb of Liverpool. Even so, problems persist with Gundahari's center at Worms, a city that cannot really be called anything else. Generations of English-speaking school children have derived innocent amusement at the expense of a fine city in phrases like "the Diet of Worms"; but Gerwit in the poem is an Earl ("Count" is not an English title) of Worms, so that all conceivable echoes of proverbs about early birds catching worms must be circumvented if possible. Beyond that, all a translator can do is make an initial plea that the town be pronounced (even mentally) as in German, with an initial [v] and a rounded vowel.

More generally, the poet makes frequent use of *is(te)* and *ille*, especially in fights, and we have often added in names to make clear precisely who is doing what. Equally, with a few exceptions where the text is particularly exciting, the historic present has been avoided. We have aimed at line-for-line translations, but sometimes this has not been possible, either for reasons of sense (where the Latin is very concise) or more rarely to make a poetic point. We have also tried to avoid too many iterative forms.

There have been other translations of the work in prose and verse in German, English, French, and other languages (even via the version in Scheffel's novel). Of those in English, the most recent is the prose translation by Ring (2016), which exhibits a number of virtues, though its utility and legibility are marred considerably by its author's decision to render all Greek-derived vocabulary into French—a decision justly criticized by Wieland (2019) in his review. Ring's introduction and notes, however, are rich and learned, and certainly worth consulting. For an English prose translation that aims to be strictly literal, and clearly prioritizes the literal over the readable, one can turn to Magoun & Smyser (1950). Of the available verse translations, Jones's (1950) incomplete pentameter version is interesting for its occasional veering into Victorian-medieval diction; it contains some first-rate lines, as when the Huns, made drunk by Walthari, become incoherent "and bib'lous throats spout fuddled eloquence." The verse translation by Kratz (1984) is generally accurate and legible, with some appealing renderings (e.g., "voracious lust of having" in l. 857) and others that are less appealing. He provides the reader with very few notes on *Waltharius*, supplying instead an edition and translation

INTRODUCTION

of *Ruodlieb*. The font and formatting used in the production of Kratz's text are, it must be said, inexplicably hideous.

Every translation is questionable in places, and there are problems which do not admit of a definite answer, and here too, of course, *ad hoc* decisions have had to be made on difficult passages for the sake of a readable text. Debate will doubtless continue on some of those passages (such as the *Franci nebulones* in line 555 or the *celtica lingua* in line 765). In German, one of the most readily available (and very good) texts was that produced by Felix Genzmer (1953) for Reclam, originally firmly ascribed to Ekkehard, but whose name has disappeared from the cover of the more recent reprints. The usefulness of Genzmer's text is here readily acknowledged, with all the English translations named above. It is divided neatly into twelve sections described in *Nibelungen*-fashion as *Abenteuer* (an idea borrowed, he tells us [1953: 59], from Hermann Althof's 1905 edition of the poem). To these must be added not only the translation which accompanied Strecker's 1947 edition (by Peter Vossen), but what is probably the best German version, and one which uses a convincingly Germanic-looking, often alliterative long line divided by a caesura, that of Karl Langosch (1956), now available in an attractive *Insel*-edition, a parallel text, with Ekkehard's name still in pride of place. Langosch also divides the work up into chapters.

The text of *Waltharius* has become more or less fixed in modern scholarship. Editions tend to exhibit only minor differences, and they tend to agree on most contestable readings with the *editio maior* of Karl Strecker, the *Monumenta Germaniae Historica* version completed by Strecker in 1943 and published in 1951, five years after his death. Strecker's edition, however, does not print Gerald's prologue, which had already appeared in an earlier volume of *Monumenta Germaniae Historica*. The prologue is printed, though, in the more recent editions that we have consulted, such as Bate (1978), Kratz (1984), and Ring (2016). The text of *Waltharius* printed here, upon which the translation is based, includes the prologue and, like the other recent editions, features only a handful of minor deviations from Strecker (1951), which are discussed in the notes. Our notes are not primarily concerned with disputed readings—the *apparatus criticus* in Ring (2016) does a fine job of cataloguing variants—but are concerned rather with the interpretation and contextualization of the poem. Asterisks are used throughout to indicate words, passages, or personages discussed in the notes.

BIBLIOGRAPHY

This bibliography is intended to provide, in addition to a list of works cited and consulted, a concise overview for the reader interested in learning more about *Waltharius* and other works and topics mentioned in the introduction. There is a preference throughout for recent works and works written in English. What follows, it should be stressed, is selective rather than comprehensive. The amount of secondary literature on *Waltharius* and the Walther tradition is enormous, and more has been written on these subjects in German than in English. A good deal of German scholarship is therefore present in this bibliography as well.

PRIMARY TEXTS

1. **Editions of *Waltharius***

BATE, Alan K. *Waltharius of Gaeraldus*. Reading: Department of Classics, University of Reading, 1978.

KRATZ, Dennis M. *Waltharius and Ruodlieb*. New York: Garland Publishing, 1984.

LANGOSCH, Karl. *Waltharius: Lateinisch und deutsch.* Leipzig: Insel Verlag, 1988.

LEARNED, Marion Dexter. *The Saga of Walther of Aquitaine.* Baltimore: Modern Language Association of America, 1892.

RING, Abram. *Waltharius.* Leuven: Peeters, 2016.

STRECKER, Karl. *Waltharius.* Deutsche Übersetzung von Peter VOSSEN. Berlin: Weidmann, 1947.

STRECKER, Karl. *Nachträge zu den Poetae Aevi Carolini I.* Weimar: Böhlau, 1951.

WIELAND, Gernot. *Waltharius.* Bryn Mawr: Thomas Library, 1986.

2. Translations of *Waltharius*

GENZMER, Felix. *Das Waltharilied.* Stuttgart: Reclam, 1953 (repr. 1994).

LANGOSCH: see above, section 1.

JONES, Charles W. *Medieval Literature in Translation.* New York: McKay, 1950. [partial English verse translation]

KRATZ: see above, section 1.

MAGOUN, F. P., Jr., & SMYSER, H.M. *Walter of Aquitaine. Materials for the Study of His Legend.* New London, CT: Connecticut College, 1950.

RING: see above, section 1.

BIBLIOGRAPHY

SMYSER, H, M. & MAGOUN, F. P., Jr. *Survivals in Old Norwegian of Medieval English, French and German Literature together with the Latin versions of the Heroic Legend of Walter of Aquitaine*. Baltimore: Waverly Press, 1941.

VOSSEN: see above, section 1, STRECKER (1947).

3. Other Primary Works

Analogues (other than Waldere)

LEARNED: see above, section 1. Reprints *Waldere*, the *Chronicon Novaliciense*, the Graz and Vienna Fragments, the passages from *Þiðreks saga* in Old Norse and Old Swedish, the *Boguphali Chronicon* (*Wielkopolska Kronika*), Procopius, and four Polish texts, as well as relevant extracts from Walther von der Vogelweide, the *Nibelungenlied*, and the Dietrich epics. The collection includes—again in the original—passages naming Walther/Gualt(i)er in the French and German Roland poems and *Von dem übelen wibe*.

MAGOUN & SMYSER: see above, section 2. Translations of *Waldere*, *Chronicon Novaliciense*, the Graz and Vienna fragments, *Þiðreks saga*, and the Polish material.

MURDOCH, Brian & NEIDORF, Leonard. *The Legend of Walther of Aquitaine: Medieval German Texts and Translations*. London: Uppsala Books (forthcoming).

SCHWAB: see below, *Waldere*. Includes texts of *Þiðreks saga*, MHG fragments (with manuscript photographs), Polish-Latin Chronicle, *Chronicon Novaliciense*.

Beowulf

FULK, R.D., BJORK, Robert E., & NILES, John D. *Klaeber's Beowulf: Fourth Edition*. Toronto: University of Toronto Press, 2008.

SHIPPEY, Tom & NEIDORF, Leonard. *Beowulf: Translation and Commentary: Revised and Expanded*. London: Uppsala Books, 2024.

Chanson de Roland

BRAULT, Gerald J. *The Song of Roland: An Analytical Edition*. 2 vols. University Park: Pennsylvania State University Press, 1978.

GAUNT, Simon & PRATT, Karen. *The Song of Roland and other Poems of Charlemagne*. Oxford: Oxford University Press, 2017.

Kudrun

BARTSCH, K. *Kudrun*. 5th ed., rev. by K. STACKMANN. Tübingen: Max Niemeyer Verlag, 2000.

MURDOCH, Brian O. *Kudrun*. London: Dent, 1987.

Medieval Latin Poetry

DÜMMLER, Ernst. *Poetae Latini Aevi Carolini*. Vol. 1. Berlin: Weidmann, 1881.

DÜMMLER, Ernst. *Poetae Latini Aevi Carolini*. Vol. 2. Berlin: Weidmann, 1884.

GODMAN, Peter. *Poetry of the Carolingian Renaissance*. London: Duckworth, 1985. [Translates brief extracts of *Waltharius*, pp. 326-41]

LANGOSCH, Karl. *Lyrische Anthologie des lateinischen Mittelalters.* Darmstadt: Wissenschaftliche Buchgesellschaft, 1968.

RABY, F. J. E. *The Oxford Book of Medieval Latin Verse.* Oxford: Clarendon, 1959.

WADDELL, Helen. *Medieval Latin Lyrics.* Harmondsworth: Penguin, 1952.

WADDELL, Helen. *More Latin Lyrics.* London: Gollancz, 1980.

Nibelungenlied

BARTSCH, K. rev. de BOOR, H., *Das Nibelungenlied*, 21 ed. revised by Roswitha WISNIEWSKI. Wiesbaden: Brockhaus, 1979.

EDWARDS, Cyril. *The Nibelungenlied: The Lay of the Nibelungs.* Oxford: Oxford University Press, 2010.

Scheffel

SCHEFFEL, Joseph Victor von. *Ekkehard. Eine Geschichte aus dem zehnten Jahrhundert* [Frankfurt/M.: Meidinger, 2. vols., 1855]. Stuttgart: Bonz, 1904.

SCHEFFEL, Joseph Victor von. *Ekkehard*, trans. Helena EASSON. London: Dent, 1906. [translation of *Waltharius* in Chapter 241]

Vergil

LEWIS, C. DAY. *The Eclogues, Georgics, and Aeneid of Virgil.* London: Oxford University Press, 1966.

MYNORS, R. A. B. *P. Vergili Maronis Opera.* Oxford: Clarendon Press, 1969.

Vǫlundarkviða (Old Norse Song of Wayland)

LARRINGTON, Carolyne. *The Poetic Edda*. Oxford: Oxford University Press, 2014.

NECKEL, Gustav. *Edda: Die Lieder des Codex Regius nebst verwandten Denkmälern*. 2 vols. 5th ed. rev. by Hans Kuhn. Heidelberg: Carl Winter, 1983.

Waldere

ALEXANDER, Michael. *The Earliest English Poems*. Harmondsworth: Penguin, 1966.

GENZMER: see above, section 1.

HIMES, Jonathan B. *The Old English Epic of Waldere*. Newcastle upon Tyne: Cambridge Scholars Publishing, 2009.

NORMAN, F. *Waldere*. 2nd ed. London: Methuen, 1949.

SCHWAB, Ute. *Waldere*. Messina: Libreria Peloritana, 1967.

ZETTERSTEN, Arne. *Waldere*. Manchester: Manchester University Press, 1979.

SECONDARY STUDIES

4. Heroic Literature

BOWRA, C. M. *From Virgil to Milton*. London: Macmillan, 1945.

BOWRA, C. M. *Heroic Poetry*. London: Macmillan, 1964.

BIBLIOGRAPHY

CHADWICK, H. M. *The Heroic Age*. Cambridge: Cambridge University Press, 1912.

CURTIUS, Ernst Robert. *European Literature and the Latin Middle Ages*, trans. Willard R. TRASK [1953], with a new introduction by Colin BURROW. Princeton: Princeton University Press, 2013.

DE BOOR, Helmut. *Das Attilabild in Geschichte, Legende und heroischer Dichtung*. Reprint edition. Darmstadt: Wissenschaftliche Buchgesellschaft, 1963.

GENTRY, Francis G., MCCONNELL, Winder, MÜLLER, Ulrich, & WUNDERLICH, Werner. *The Nibelungen Tradition: An Encyclopedia*. New York: Routledge, 2002.

GILLESPIE, George T. *A Catalogue of Persons Named in German Heroic Literature*, 700-1600. Oxford: Clarendon, 1973.

HAUG, Walther. "Mittelalterliche Epik: Ansätze, Brechungen und Perspektiven." In *Epische Stoffe des Mittelalters*, ed. Volker MERTENS and Ulrich MÜLLER (pp. 1-19). Stuttgart: Kroner, 1984.

JACKSON, W. T. H. *The Hero and the King: An Epic Theme*. New York: Columbia University Press, 1982.

KER, W. P. *Epic and Romance: Essays on Medieval Literature* [1908]. New York: Dover, 1957.

LAISTNER, M. L. W. *Thought and Letters in Western Europe, AD 500-900*. Rev. ed. London: Methuen.

MURDOCH, Brian. *The Germanic Hero: Politics and Pragmatism in Early Medieval Poetry*. London: Hambledon Press, 1996.

NEIDORF, Leonard. "Hrothgar and Etzel: *Beowulf* Analogues in Middle High German Literature." *English Studies* 104 (2023): 1317-32.

TOLKIEN, J. R. R. "*Beowulf*: The Monsters and the Critics." *Proceedings of the British Academy* (1936): 245-95.

UECKER, Heiko. *Germanische Heldensage*. Stuttgart: Metzler, 1972.

von SEE, Klaus. *Germanische Heldensage*. Frankfurt/M.: Athenaeum, 1971.

de VRIES, Jan. *Heroic Song and Heroic Legend*, trans. B. J. TIMMER. London: Oxford University Press, 1963.

5. *Waltharius*

BECKMANN, Gustav A. *Gualter del Hum – Gaiferos – Waltharius*. Berlin: de Gruyter, 2010.

BLASCHKA, Anton. "Eine Versuchsreihe zum *Waltharius*-Problem." *Wissenschaftliche Zeitschrift der Martin-Luther-Universität Halle-Wittenberg* 5 (1956): 413-19.

BLASCHKA, Anton. "Zweite Versuchsreihe zum *Waltharius*-Problem." *Wissenschaftliche Zeitschrift der Martin-Luther-Universität Halle-Wittenberg* 11 (1962): 1539-42.

BORNHOLDT, Claudia. *Engaging Moments: The Origins of Medieval Bridal-Quest Narrative*. Berlin: de Gruyter, 2005.

BRINKMANN, Hennig. "Ekkehards *Waltharius* als Kunstwerk." *Zeitschrift für deutsche Bildung* 4 (1928): 625-36.

BIBLIOGRAPHY

CARROLL, Jr., Benjamin H. "An Essay on the Walther Legend." *Florida State University Studies* 5 (1952): 123-79.

CARROLL, Jr., Benjamin H. "On the Lineage of the Walther Legend." *Germanic Review* 28 (1953): 34-41.

CLASSEN, Albrecht. "An Ecocritical Reading of an Early Medieval Heroic Epic: *Walthariuslied/Waltharius*." *Sankalp Journal of Multidisciplinary Studies* 4 (2024): 5-19.

CLASSEN, Carl Joachim. "Beobachtungen zum *Waltharius*: Die gegen Walther gerichteten Scheltreden." *Mittellateinisches Jahrbuch* 21 (1986): 75-8.

DRONKE, Peter. "Waltharius-Gaiferos." In *Barbara et antiquissima carmina*, ed. Peter & Ursula DRONKE (pp. 27-79). Barcelona: Universidad Autónoma de Barcelona, 1977.

DUMVILLE, David. "Ekiurid's 'Celtica lingua': An Ethnological Difficulty in *Waltharius*." *Cambridge Medieval Celtic Studies* 6 (1983): 87-93.

EIS, Gerhard. "*Waltharius*-Probleme." In *Britannica: Festschrift für Hermann M. Flasdieck*, ed. Wolfgang ISER & Hans SCHABRAM (pp. 96-112). Heidelberg: Winter, 1960.

EBELING-KONING, Blanche T. *Style and Structure in Ekkehard's Waltharius*. PhD Dissertation: Columbia University, 1977.

ERNST, Ursula. "Walther – ein christlicher Held?" *Mittellateinisches Jahrbuch* 21 (1986): 79-83.

FICKERMANN, Norbert. "Zum Verfasserproblem des *Waltharius*." *Beiträge zur Geschichte der deutschen Sprache und Literatur* 81 (1959): 267-73.

FLATT, Tyler. "The Book of Friends: Hagen and Heroic Traditions in the *Waltharius*." *Journal of English and Germanic Philology* 115 (2016): 463-85.

GABE, Sabine. "Gefolgschaft und Blutrache im *Waltharius*." *Mittellateinisches Jahrbuch* 21(1986): 91-94.

GARLAND, Henry & Mary. *The Oxford Companion to German Literature*. Oxford: Oxford University Press, 1976.

GENZMER, Felix. "Wie der *Waltharius* entstanden ist." *Germanisch-romanische Monatsschrift* 35 (1954): 161-78.

GILLESPIE, George. "The Significance of Personal Names in German Heroic Poetry." In *Medieval German Studies Presented to Frederick Norman* (pp. 16-21). London: Institute of Germanic Studies, 1965.

GRÉGOIRE, Henri. "La Patrie des Nibelungen." *Byzantion* 9 (1934): 1-39.

GRÉGOIRE, Henri. "Le *Waltharius* et Strasbourg." *Bulletin de la Faculté des Lettres de Strasbourg* 14 (1936): 201-13.

HAEFELE, Hans-Friedrich. "*Vita Waltharii manufortis*." In *Festschrift Bernhard Bischoff*, ed. Johannes AUTENRIETH & Franz BRUNHÖLZL (pp. 260-76). Stuttgart: Hiersemann, 1971.

HARMS, Wolfgang. *Der Kampf mit dem Freund oder Verwandten in der deutschen Literatur bis um 1300*. Munich: Fink, 1963.

HAUCK, Karl. "Das Walthariusepos des Bruders Gerald von Eichstätt." *Germanisch-Romanische Monatsschrifte* 35 (1954): 1-27.

BIBLIOGRAPHY

HEINTZE, Michael. "Gualter del Hum in *Rolandslied*: Zur Romanisierung der Walther-Sage." *Mittellateinisches Jahrbuch* 21 (1986): 95-100.

JONES, George F. "The Ethos of the *Waltharius*." In *Middle Ages, Reformation, Volkskunde: Festschrift for John G. Kunstmann*, ed. Frederic E. COENEN (pp. 1-20). Chapel Hill: University of North Carolina Press, 1959.

JONES, George F. "The *Celtica Lingua* Spoken in the *Saxonicis Oris*: Concerning *Waltharius* vv. 756-780." *Germanic Review* 49 (1974): 17-22.

KLOPSCH, Paul. "Der Waltharius." *Der altsprachliche Unterricht* 6 (1963): 45-62.

KRATZ, Dennis M. *Mocking Epic: Waltharius, Alexandreis and the Problem of Christian Heroism*. Madrid: José Porrúa Turanzas, 1980.

KROES, H. W. J. "Die Walthersage." *Beiträge zur Geschichte der deutschen Sprache und Literatur* 77 (1955): 77-88.

LANGOSCH, Karl. "*Waltharius*." In *Die deutsche Literatur des Mittelalters: Verfasserlexikon*, vol. 4, ed. Wolfgang STAMMLER & Karl LANGOSCH (pp. 776-88). Berlin: de Gruyter, 1953.

LANGOSCH, Karl. "Die Vorlage des *Waltharius*." In *Festschrift Bernhard Bischoff*, ed. Johannes AUTENRIETH & Franz BRUNHÖLZL (pp. 226-59). Stuttgart: Hiersemann, 1971.

LANGOSCH, Karl. *Waltharius: Die Dichtung und die Forschung*. Darmstadt: Wissenschaftliche Buchgesellschaft, 1973.

LANGOSCH, Karl. "Zum *Waltharius* Ekkeharts I. von St Gallen." *Mittellateinisches Jahrbuch* 18 (1983): 84-99.

LÜHRS, Maria. "Hiltgunt." *Mittellateinisches Jahrbuch* 21 (1986): 84-7.

MACLEAN, Simon. "*Waltharius*: Treasure, Revenge and Kingship in the Ottonian Wild West." In *Emotion, Violence, Vengeance and Law in the Middle Ages*, ed. Kate GILBERT & Stephen D. WHITE (pp. 225-51). Leiden: Brill, 2018.

MAKKAY, János. *Iranian Elements in Early Mediaeval Heroic Poetry: the Arthurian Cycle and the Waltharius*. Budapest: J. Makkay, 1998.

MILLET, Victor. "*Waltharius* and the *Chanson de Roland*: A Survey." In *Aspects de l'épopée romane: Mentalités - idéologies – intertextualités*, ed. Hans van DIJK & Willem NOOMEN (pp. 391-97). Groningen: Forsten, 1995.

MORGAN, Gareth. "Walther the Wood-Sprite." *Medium Aevum* 41 (1972): 16-19.

MÜNKLER, Herfried. *Das Blickfeld des Helden: Zur Darstellung des Römischen Reichs in der germanisch-deutschen Heldendichtung*. Göppingen: Kümmerle, 1983.

NEIDORF, Leonard. "Goths, Huns, and *The Dream of the Rood*." *Review of English Studies* 72 (2021): 821-35.

OLSEN, Alexandra Hennessey. "Formulaic Tradition and the Latin *Waltharius*." In *Heroic Poetry in the Anglo-Saxon Period: Studies in Honor of Jess B. Bessinger Jr.*, ed. Helen DAMICO & John LEYERLE (pp. 265-82). Kalamazoo: Medieval Institute, 1993.

ÖNNERFORS, Alf. *Die Verfasserschaft des Waltharius-Epos aus sprachlicher Sicht*. Opladen: Westdeutscher Verlag, 1979.

PANZER, Friedrich. *Der Kampf am Wasichenstein: Waltharius-Studien.* Speyer am Rhein: Verlag Historisches Museum der Pfalz, 1948.

PANZER, Friedrich. "*Waltharius* in neuer Beleuchtung." *Forschungen und Fortschritte* 24 (1948): 156-58.

PARKES, Ford B. "Irony in *Waltharius*." *MLN* 89 (1974): 459-65.

PLOSS, Emil Ernst. *Waltharius und Walthersage – Eine Dokumentation der Forschung.* Hildesheim: Olms, 1969.

RENOIR, Alain. "*Nibelungenlied* and *Waltharii poesis*: A Note on Tragic Irony." *Philological Quarterly* 43 (1964): 14-19.

RIO, Alice. "*Waltharius* at Fontenoy? Epic Heroism and Carolingian Political Thought." *Viator* 46 (2015): 41-64.

SCHALLER, Dieter. "Ist der *Waltharius* frühkarolingisch?" *Mittellateinisches Jahrbuch* 18 (1983): 63-83.

SCHERELLO, Bernd. "Die Darstellung Gunthers im *Waltharius*." *Mittellateinisches Jahrbuch* 21 (1986): 88-90.

SCHIEFFER, Rudolf. "Zu neuen Thesen über den *Waltharius*." *Deutsches Archiv für Erforschung des Mittelalters* 36 (1980): 193-201.

SCHNEIDER, Hermann. "Das Epos von Walther und Hildegund." *Germanisch-Romanische Monatsschrifte* 13 (1925): 14-32, 119-30.

SCHUHMANN, Otto. "Zum *Waltharius*." *Zeitschrift für deutsches Altertum* 83 (1951): 12-40.

SCHUHMANN, Otto. "*Waltharius*-Literatur seit 1926." *Anzeiger für deutsches Altertum* 65 (1951-52): 13-41.

SCHÜTTE, Bernd. "Länder und Völker im *Waltharius*." *Mittellateinisches Jahrbuch* 21 (1986): 70-74.

STACH, Walter, "Geralds *Waltharius*, das erste Heldenepos der Deutschen." *Historische Zeitschrift* 168 (1943): 57-81.

von den STEINEN, Wolfram. "Der *Waltharius* und sein Dichter." *Zeitschrift für deutsches Altertum* 84 (1952-53): 1-47.

STONE, Rachel. "*Waltharius* and Carolingian Morality: Satire and Lay Values." *Early Medieval Europe* 21 (2013): 50-70.

SURLES, Robert L. *Roots and Branches: Germanic Epic / Romanic Legend.* New York: Peter Lang, 1987.

SÜSS, Gustav Adolf. "Die Probleme der *Waltharius*-Forschung." *Zeitschrift für Geschichte des Oberreins* 99 (1951): 1-53.

TAVERNIER, Wilhelm. "*Waltharius*, *Carmen de prodicione Guenonis* und *Rolandsepos*." *Zeitschrift für französische Sprache und Literatur* 42 (1914): 41-81.

TOWNSEND, David. "Ironic Intertextuality and the Reader's Resistance to Heroic Masculinity in the *Waltharius*." In *Becoming Male in the Middle Ages*, ed. Jeffrey Jerome COHEN & Bonnie WHEELER (pp. 67-86). New York: Garland, 1997.

TURCAN-VERKERK, Anne-Marie. "La Diffusion du *Waltharius* et son Anonymat: Essai d'Interprétation." *Filologia Mediolatina* 23 (2016): 59-122.

WARD, John O. "After Rome: Medieval Epic." In *Roman Epic*, ed. A.J. BOYLE (pp. 261-93). London: Routledge, 1993.

WEHRLI, Max. "*Waltharius*: Gattungsgeschichtliche Betrachtungen." *Mittellateinisches Jahrbuch* 2 (1965): 63-73.

WERNER, Karl-Ferdinand. "Hludowicus Augustus: Gouverner l'empire chrétien – Idées et réalités." In *Charlemagne's Heir: New Perspectives on the Reign of Louis the Pious (814-840)*, ed. Peter GODMAN & Roger COLLINS (pp. 3-123). Oxford: Clarendon Press, 1990.

WESTRA, Haijo Jan. "A Reinterpretation of *Waltharius* 215-259." *Mittellateinisches Jahrbuch* 15 (1980): 51-6.

WIELAND, Gernot. "Review of RING 2016." *Speculum* 94 (2019): 274-5.

WOLF, Alfred. "Der mittellateinische *Waltharius* und Ekkehard von St. Gallen." *Studia Neophilologica* 13 (1940-41): 80-102.

WOLF, Alfred. "Zum Waltharius christianus." *Zeitschrift für deutsches Altertum* 85 (1954-55): 291-93.

ZEYDEL, Edwin H. "Prologomena to an English translation of *Waltharius*." In *Middle Ages, Reformation, Volkskunde: Festschrift for John G. Kunstmann*, ed. Frederic E. COENEN (pp. 21-38). Chapel Hill: University of North Carolina Press, 1959.

ZIOLKOWSKI, Jan M. Review of KRATZ 1980. *Classical Journal* 78 (1983): 266-8.

ZIOLKOWSKI, Jan M. "Fighting Words: Wordplay and Swordplay in the *Waltharius*." In *Germanic Texts and Latin Models: Medieval Reconstructions*, ed. K.E. OLSEN, A. HARBUS & T. HOFSTRA (pp. 29-52). Leuven: Peeters, 2001.

ZIOLKOWSKI, Jan M. "Of Arms and the (Ger)man: Literary and Material Culture in the *Waltharius*." In *The Long Morning of Medieval Europe: New Directions in Early Medieval Studies*, ed. Jennifer R. DAVIS & Michael MCCORMICK (pp. 193-208). London: Routledge, 2008.

ZIOLKOWSKI, Jan M. "Walther of Aquitaine in Spanish Ballad Tradition." In *Child's Children: Ballad Study and its Legacies*, ed. Joseph HARRIS & Barbara HILLERS (pp. 171-85). Trier: Wissenschaftlicher Verlag Trier, 2012.

ZWIERLEIN, Otto. "Das *Waltharius*-Epos und seine lateinischen Vorbilder." *Antike und Abendland* 16 (1970): 153-84.

6. Other Secondary Studies

Classical and Medieval Latin

BOLGAR, R. R. *The Classical Heritage and its Beneficiaries*. Cambridge: Cambridge University Press, 1954.

LANGOSCH, Karl. *Mittellateinische Dichtung*. Darmstadt: Wissenschaftliche Buchgesellschaft, 1969.

LANGOSCH, Karl. *Lateinisches Mittelalter: Einführung in Sprache und Literatur*. Darmstadt: Wissenschaftliche Buchgesellschaft, 1975.

MANITIUS, Max. *Geschichte der lateinischen Literatur des Mittelalters*. Munich: Beck, 1911-31.

RABY, Frederick J. *A History of Secular Latin Poetry in the Middle Ages*. 2 vols. 2nd ed. Oxford: Clarendon, 1957.

WILLIAMS, R. Deryck. *Aeneas and the Roman Hero*. London: Macmillan, 1973.

WRIGHT, F. A. & SINCLAIR, T. A. *A History of Later Latin Literature*. London: Routledge, 1931.

On Translation

GRIERSON, Herbert J.C. *Verse Translation with Special Reference to Translation from the Latin.* London: Oxford University Press, 1948.

RADICE, William & REYNOLDS, Barbara. *The Translator's Art: Essays in Honour of Betty Radice.* Harmondsworth: Penguin, 1987.

History

BROWN, Peter. *Through the Eye of a Needle: Wealth, the Fall of Rome, and the Making of Christianity in the West, 350-550 AD.* Princeton: Princeton University Press, 2013.

FLYNN, Christopher P. "Fontenoy and the Justification of Battle-Seeking Strategy in the Ninth Century." *Mediaevistik* 35 (2022): 89-110.

GHOSH, Shami. *Writing the Barbarian Past: Studies in Early Medieval Historical Narrative.* Leiden: Brill, 2016.

KENT, J. P. C. & PAINTER, K. S. *Wealth of the Roman World: Gold and Silver AD 300-700.* London: British Museum, 1977.

MCKITTERICK, Rosamund. *Charlemagne: The Formation of a European Identity.* Cambridge: Cambridge University Press, 2008.

THOMPSON, E. A. *The Early Germans.* Oxford: Clarendon, 1965.

WALLACE-HADRILL, J. M. *The Barbarian West, 400-1000.* 3rd ed. London: Hutchinson, 1967.

WALTHARIUS

The Latin Epic of Walther of Aquitaine

PROLOGUS GERALDI

    Omnipotens genitor, summae virtutis amator,
    Iure pari natusque amborum spiritus almus,
    Personis trinus, vera deitate sed unus,
    Qui vita vivens cuncta et sine fine tenebis,
5 Pontificem summum tu salva nunc et in aevum
    Claro Erckambaldum fulgentem nomine dignum,
    Crescat ut interius sancto spiramine plenus,
    Multis infictum quo sit medicamen in aevum.

    Praesul sancte dei, nunc accipe munera servi,
10 Quae tibi decrevit de larga promere cura
    Peccator fragilis Geraldus nomine vilis,
    Qui tibi nam certus corde estque fidelis alumnus.
    Quod precibus dominum iugiter precor omnitonantem,
    Ut nanciscaris factis, quae promo loquelis,
15 Det pater ex summis caelum terramque gubernans.

    Serve dei summi, ne despice verba libelli,
    Non canit alma dei, resonat sed mira tyronis,
    Nomine Waltharius, per proelia multa resectus.
    Ludendum magis est dominum quam sit rogitandum,
20 Perlectus longaevi stringit inampla diei.
    Sis felix sanctus per tempora plura sacerdos,
    Sit tibi mente tua Geraldus carus adelphus.

TRANSLATION

GERALD'S PROLOGUE

O God omnipotent, Christ, in virtues content,
and Thou, equal of both, beloved Holy Ghost,
in persons a Trinity, united in true Divinity
eternally to tend the whole world without end,
preserve now and for aye my Lord Bishop, the most high
Erkambald, a man illustrious in status,
that he may grow a pace in the Holy Ghost's grace,
ever a true medicine for those irked* by sin.

Holy Bishop of the Lord, receive a servant's words,
brought out with zealous care,* and laid before you here
by a sinner full of shame, Gerald* by name,
who, wholehearted and sure, is your true follower.
With all my prayers I implore God the Thunderer*
to let you carry out the things I speak about;
Father, ruler of all you see from High Heaven, let it be!

O servant of God on high! My little book do not despise!
Its theme is not God's glory, but a young man's story—
Walthari, a warrior much wounded in war.
Its aim is to delight, not to point the path to Christ!
When read through, my song shortens days that are too long!
Be happy as God's minister for many a year!
May Gerald, your brother,* be remembered lovingly.

WALTHARIUS

    Tertia pars orbis, fratres, Europa vocatur,
    Moribus ac linguis varias et nomine gentes
    Distinguens cultu, tum relligione sequestrans.
    Inter quas gens Pannoniae residere probatur,
5 Quam tamen et Hunos plerumque vocare solemus.
    Hic populus fortis virtute vigebat et armis,
    Non circumpositas solum domitans regiones,
    Litoris oceani sed pertransiverat oras,
    Foedera supplicibus donans sternensque rebelles.
10 Ultra millenos fertur dominarier annos.

    Attila rex quodam tulit illud tempore regnum,
    Impiger antiquos sibimet renovare triumphos.
    Qui sua castra movens mandavit visere Francos,
    Quorum rex Gibicho solio pollebat in alto,
15 Prole recens orta gaudens, quam postea narro:
    Namque marem genuit, quem Guntharium vocitavit.

    Fama volans pavidi regis transverberat aures,
    Dicens hostilem cuneum transire per Hystrum,
    Vincentem numero stellas atque amnis arenas.
20 Qui non confidens armis vel robore plebis
    Concilium cogit, quae sint facienda, requirit.
    Consensere omnes foedus debere precari
    Et dextras, si forte darent, coniungere dextris

TRANSLATION

WALTHARIUS

The third part of this earth, brothers, is called Europe,*
its many peoples set apart by customs, names, and tongues,
distinguished also by their gods and their beliefs.
Amongst them all, Pannonia's* men are greatly famed—
a nation known to us by the name of Huns,
a fierce and warlike people, bold and strong in arms.
Not only did they conquer all their neighboring lands,
but fought their way towards the Western Ocean, offering
alliance to all who wished it; war, if they would not.
They ruled for longer than a thousand years.

King Attila* at one time ruled that kingdom,
and strove without respite to match his early triumphs.
He gave an order to besiege and to attack the Franks,
whose high king, Gibicho,* ruled then with sovereign power,
rejoicing in a newborn son (of whom we shall hear more)—
Gibicho had an heir. He named him Gundahari.

Disturbing news, carried on the wind, came to the king.
Enemies from across the Danube had moved in, he heard,
more numerous than stars at night or grains of sand.
Gibicho trusted neither to his weapons nor his forces,
and so he sought advice on his best course of action.
All counsellors agreed that he should seek alliance
and that, if it were offered, he should take the hand

Obsidibusque datis censum persolvere iussum;
25 Hoc melius fore quam vitam simul ac regionem
Perdiderint natosque suos pariterque maritas.

Nobilis hoc Hagano fuerat sub tempore tiro
Indolis egregiae, veniens de germine Troiae.
Hunc, quia Guntharius nondum pervenit ad aevum,
30 Ut sine matre queat vitam retinere tenellam,
Cum gaza ingenti decernunt mittere regi.
Nec mora, legati censum iuvenemque ferentes
Deveniunt pacemque rogant ac foedera firmant.

Tempore quo validis steterat Burgundia sceptris,
35 Cuius primatum Heriricus forte gerebat.
Filia huic tantum fuit unica nomine Hiltgunt,
Nobilitate quidem pollens ac stemmate formae.
Debuit haec heres aula residere paterna
Atque diu congesta frui, si forte liceret.
40 Namque Avares firma cum Francis pace peracta
Suspendunt a fine quidem regionis eorum.
Attila sed celeres mox huc deflectit habenas,
Nec tardant reliqui satrapae vestigia adire.
Ibant aequati numero, sed et agmine longo,
45 Quadrupedum cursu tellus concussa gemebat.
Scutorum sonitu pavidus superintonat aether.
Ferrea silva micat totos rutilando per agros:
Haud aliter primo quam pulsans aequora mane
Pulcher in extremis renitet sol partibus orbis.
50 Iamque Ararim Rodanumque amnes transiverat altos
Atque ad praedandum cuneus dispergitur omnis.

Forte Cabillonis sedit Heriricus, et ecce
Attollens oculos speculator vociferatur:
'Quaenam condenso consurgit pulvere nubes?
55 Vis inimica venit, portas iam claudite cunctas!'

of peace, should offer hostages and pay the tribute asked.
Far better this, than they should lose their lands and lives,
and that their women and their children should be taken.

In those days there lived a noble boy called Hagano,*
descended from the Trojans, of flawless lineage.
Since Gundahari was not of an age at which he could
survive without his mother, it was agreed
that Hagano be sent to Attila with much gold. This was done
without delay. Envoys took the treasure and the boy,
they sued for peace with Attila, established an alliance.

At this time the Burgundians,* too, enjoyed firm rule,
under the scepter of their king, Heririk.
His only daughter was called Hildigunda, a girl
as beautiful as she was nobly born. The intention was
that she should live as heiress in her father's hall
if life were granted to her. But once the Huns*
had settled their peace-treaty with the Franks
they moved out to the borders of their lands.
When Attila turned his horse and rode away,
his satraps were not slow to follow in his path.
Ordered they marched, a great column of warriors.
Their horses' hoofbeats caused the very earth to groan
and the trembling air rang with the clash of shields,
an iron forest turning red the open land
just as the sun at dawn lights up the sea, a light
that is reflected back from every part of the earth.
Soon they had crossed the Saone and after that the Rhone,
and then the troops spread out in search of plunder.

Heririk was holding court at Chalon.* Suddenly
a sentry shouted, keeping lookout on the lands,
"Something has driven up a swirling cloud of dust,
an enemy force is coming! Bar all the gates!"

Iam tum, quid Franci fecissent, ipse sciebat
Princeps et cunctos compellat sic seniores:
'Si gens tam fortis, cui nos similare nequimus,
Cessit Pannoniae, qua nos virtute putatis
60 Huic conferre manum et patriam defendere dulcem?
Est satius, pactum faciant censumque capessant
Unica nata mihi, quam tradere pro regione
Non dubito: tantum pergant, qui foedera firment.

Ibant legati totis gladiis spoliati,
65 Hostibus insinuant, quod regis iussio mandat:
Ut cessent vastare, rogant, quos Attila ductor,
Ut solitus fuerat, blande suscepit et inquit:
'Foedera plus cupio quam proelia mittere vulgo.
Pace quidem Huni malunt regnare, sed armis
70 Inviti feriunt, quos cernunt esse rebelles.
Rex ad nos veniens dextram det atque resumat.'

Exivit princeps asportans innumeratos
Thesauros pactumque ferit natamque reliquit.
Pergit in exilium pulcherrima gemma parentum.

75 Postquam complevit pactum statuitque tributum,
Attila in occiduas promoverat agmina partes.
Namque Aquitanorum tunc Alphere regna tenebat,
Quem sobolem sexus narrant habuisse virilis,
Nomine Waltharium, primaevo flore nitentem.
80 Nam iusiurandum Heriricus et Alphere reges
Inter se dederant, pueros quod consociarent,
Cum primum tempus nubendi venerit illis.
Hic ubi cognovit gentes has esse domatas,
Coeperat ingenti cordis trepidare pavore,
85 Nec iam spes fuerat saevis defendier armis.
'Quid cessemus', ait, 'si bella movere nequimus?
Exemplum nobis Burgundia, Francia donant.

TRANSLATION

By then the news of what the Franks had done was known.
King Heririk summoned his council and said:
"If such a mighty nation—we cannot equal them!—
has given way to the Huns, what strength could we muster
to defend our dear homeland in pitched battle?
Better for us to make a treaty and give tribute.
My only daughter shall be sent as hostage for
our land. Let those who are to treat ride out at once.

The envoys set out, every one of them unarmed
to give the enemy the message from their king,
to beg for an end to the plundering. Attila
listened courteously to their words, and then he said:
"I wish for bonds more than battles between men,
and Huns would rather rule in peace. But they take arms
(although unwillingly) against those who rebel.
Your king may come and place his right hand in mine."

The king did so, and brought a massive tribute
of gold, sealed the alliance and gave his daughter up.
The girl, her parents' loveliest jewel, became an exile.

After the treaty and the tribute had been settled,
Attila led his armies further westwards.
Alphari* ruled the kingdom of Aquitaine,
and it is said that he had a brave young heir
called Walthari, now in the bloom of his strength.
The two kings, Heririk and Alphari, had sworn
an oath to join their children in marriage,
as soon as both of them had reached the proper age.
Now, when he heard that the others had been conquered,
a great fear came over him and troubled his heart.
He could not hope for victory by force of arms.
"Why should we delay? We cannot win the fight.
The Burgundians and the Franks have set an example

Non incusamur, si talibus aequiperamur.
Legatos mitto foedusque ferire iubebo
90 Obsidis inque vicem dilectum porrigo natum
Et iam nunc Hunis censum persolvo futurum.'
Sed quid plus remorer? dictum compleverat actis.
Tunc Avares gazis onerati denique multis
Obsidibus sumptis Haganone, Hiltgunde puella
95 Nec non Walthario redierunt pectore laeto.

Attila Pannonias ingressus et urbe receptus
Exulibus pueris magnam exhibuit pietatem
Ac veluti proprios nutrire iubebat alumnos.
Virginis et curam reginam mandat habere,
100 Ast adolescentes propriis conspectibus ambos
Semper adesse iubet, sed et artibus imbuit illos
Praesertimque iocis belli sub tempore habendis.
Qui simul ingenio crescentes mentis et aevo
Robore vincebant fortes animoque sophistas,
105 Donec iam cunctos superarent fortiter Hunos.
Militiae primos tunc Attila fecerat illos,
Sed haud immerito, quoniam, si quando moveret
Bella, per insignes isti micuere triumphos;
Idcircoque nimis princeps dilexerat ambos.
110 Virgo etiam captiva deo praestante supremo
Reginae vultum placavit et auxit amorem,
Moribus eximiis operumque industria habundans.
Postremum custos thesauris provida cunctis
Efficitur, modicumque deest, quin regnet et ipsa;
115 Nam quicquid voluit de rebus, fecit et actis.

Interea Gibicho defungitur, ipseque regno
Guntharius successit et ilico Pannoniarum
Foedera dissolvit censumque subire negavit.
Hoc ubi iam primum Hagano cognoverat exul,
120 Nocte fugam molitur et ad dominum properavit.

TRANSLATION

and we cannot be blamed for following them.
I shall send envoys, ordered to arrange a treaty,
to offer my dear son as hostage, and to set
the level of the tribute paid to the Huns."
What more is there to say? The deeds followed his words.
And now the army of the Huns, loaded with treasures,
and taking with them Hagano and Hildigunda,
and also Walthari, went home with their spirits high.

Attila reached Pannonia and his fortress,
and made the best provision for the hostage boys,
with orders to treat them as if they were his own.
He gave the young girl into the care of the queen,
but commanded that the youths should always be
within his sight. He taught them every skill himself,
but mostly those useful in the great game of war.
The young hostages grew older, and learned well,
were stronger than the strong and wiser than the wise,
until each one of them had outstripped all the Huns.
Attila made them military commanders,
and they had earned it, for, whenever he waged war,
they were the ones whose deeds would always shine.
And so King Attila came to love them both.
With God's help, the young girl, too, though hostage,
was pleasing to the queen, and gained her love,
because her industry and manners marked her out.
Eventually she had charge of all the coffers
and almost ruled in her own right; for anything
she wanted, she could make the thought reality.

Meanwhile Gibicho died, and Gundahari now
succeeded to his throne. He put aside the pact
with Attila, and would not pay the tribute.
As soon as Hagano, in exile, heard of this,
he fled at night, and returned home to his king.

Waltharius tamen ad pugnas praecesserat Hunos,
Et quocumque iret, mox prospera sunt comitata.
Ospirin elapsum Haganonem regia coniunx
Attendens domino suggessit talia dicta:
125 Provideat caveatque, precor, sollertia regis,
Ne vestri imperii labatur forte columna,
Hoc est, Waltharius vester discedat amicus,
In quo magna potestatis vis extitit huius;
Nam vereor, ne fors fugiens Haganonem imitetur,
130 Idcircoque meam perpendite nunc rationem:
Cum primum veniat, haec illi dicite verba:
"Servitio in nostro magnos plerumque labores
Passus eras ideoque scias, quod gratia nostra
Prae cunctis temet nimium dilexit amicis.
135 Quod volo plus factis te quam cognoscere dictis:
Elige de satrapis nuptam tibi Pannoniarum
Et non pauperiem propriam perpendere cures.
Amplificabo quidem valde te rure domique,
Nec quisquam, qui dat sponsam, post facta pudebit."
140 Quod si completis, illum stabilire potestis.'
Complacuit sermo regi coepitque parari.

Waltharius venit, cui princeps talia pandit,
Uxorem suadens sibi ducere; sed tamen ipse
Iam tum praemeditans, quod post compleverat actis,
145 His instiganti suggestibus obvius infit:
'Vestra quidem pietas est, quod modici famulatus
Causam conspicitis. sed quod mea segnia mentis
Intuitu fertis, numquam meruisse valerem.
Sed precor, ut servi capiatis verba fidelis:
150 Si nuptam accipiam domini praecepta secundum,
Vinciar in primis curis et amore puellae
Atque a servitio regis plerumque retardor:
Aedificare domos cultumque intendere ruris
Cogor, et hoc oculis senioris adesse moratur

TRANSLATION

Walthari still fought in the forefront of the Huns,
and good luck was with him in all he undertook.
After Hagano's flight, Ospirina,* Attila's
royal queen, went to her lord and said to him:
"May the king be on his guard, and take great care
that the mainstay of his kingdom does not fall—
that Walthari, your friend, does not try to escape,
now that all our strengths are resting upon him.
I am afraid that he might follow Hagano
in flight—so listen well now to my advice!
As soon as he returns, you must tell him this:
'You have done many great deeds in our service,
and therefore know that it is our regal grace
to hold you higher than all others in our esteem.
It is our wish to show you this in deeds, not words:
you are to choose a wife from noble Hunnish stock,
with no thought that the bride-price might be too high.
We shall provide you well with house and lands. No man
will be ashamed to give his daughter as a wife.'
Do that (said Ospirina) and we can keep him here."
These words were pleasing to the king, and he agreed.

Walthari came, and Attila told him all this,
and urged him to take a wife. But Walthari
(already planning what he later carried out)
would not agree with him. Instead he answered:
"Your kindness, sir, is great, to look this way upon
my modest deeds. But my poor services do not
deserve any honor such as this, and never can.
I ask you, though, to listen to a faithful warrior:
if I, on your command, should take a wife,
then love and care of her will tie me down,
and the service of my king take second place.
My house and my estates would occupy my mind,
keeping me from the presence of my lord, and from

155 Et solitam regno Hunorum impendere curam.
Namque voluptatem quisquis gustaverit, exin
Intolerabilius consuevit ferre labores.
Nil tam dulce mihi, quam semper inesse fideli
Obsequio domini; quare precor absque iugali
160 Me vinclo permitte meam iam ducere vitam.
Si sero aut medio noctis mihi tempore mandas,
Ad quaecumque iubes, securus et ibo paratus.
In bellis nullae persuadent cedere curae
Nec nati aut coniunx retrahentque fugamque movebunt.
165 Testor per propriam temet, pater optime, vitam
Atque per invictam nunc gentem Pannoniarum
Ut non ulterius me cogas sumere taedas.'
His precibus victus suasus rex deserit omnes,
Sperans Waltharium fugiendo recedere numquam.

170 Venerat interea satrapae certissima fama
Quandam, quae nuper superata, resistere gentem
bellum Hunis confestim inferre paratam.

Tunc ad Waltharium convertitur actio rerum.
Qui mox militiam percensuit ordine totam
175 Et bellatorum confortat corda suorum,
Hortans praeteritos semper memorare triumphos
Promittensque istos solita virtute tyrannos
Sternere et externis terrorem imponere terris.

Nec mora, consurgit sequiturque exercitus omnis.
180 Ecce locum pugnae conspexerat et numeratam
Per latos aciem campos digessit et agros.
Iamque infra iactum teli congressus uterque
Constiterat cuneus: tunc undique clamor ad auras
Tollitur, horrendam confundunt classica vocem,
185 Continuoque hastae volitant hinc indeque densae.
Fraxinus et cornus ludum miscebat in unum,

my efforts to defend the realm of the Huns.
Once a man has tasted the comfortable life,
then he is less inclined to effort than before.
Nothing would be as sweet to me as to continue
in faithful service to my lord. I beg you, let me
lead my life without the chains of marriage!
If, say, you want me for some task, even at midnight,
just ask what you will and I shall act at once!
No other worries ought to hinder me in war,
no children and no wife should make me turn and flee.
I beg by all that you hold dear, most gracious lord,
and by the never-conquered nation of the Huns
that you press me no more to take a wife."
Persuaded by these words, the king gave up his plans,
in the hope that Walthari never would take flight.

But then confirmed news came: the people of a certain
vassal state, conquered not long before, were offering
resistance to the Huns, arming themselves for war.

Matters now fell into Walthari's hands. He ordered up
the military forces with all speed. His speeches
gave the men encouragement to fight with a will,
urging them to think of future victories, and promising
that with their usual vigor they would bring defeat
upon the rebels, and terror to their far-off lands.

No more ado! Walthari now rode out with all his men.
His expert eye surveyed the battle-ground, then he drew
up his battle lines on the broad fields and farmland.
Then the two vanguard forces stood within a spear-throw
of each other; battle cries re-echoed all around,
mixed with the terrifying trumpet-sounds of war,
while from all sides the spears flew thick and fast.
Spear-shafts of ash and cherry-wood clashed in that game,

Fulminis inque modum cuspis vibrata micabat.
Ac veluti boreae sub tempore nix glomerata
Spargitur, haud aliter saevas iecere sagittas.
190 Postremum cunctis utroque ex agmine pilis
Absumptis manus ad mucronem vertitur omnis:
Fulmineos promunt enses clipeosque revolvunt,
Concurrunt acies demum pugnamque restaurant.
Pectoribus partim rumpuntur pectora equorum,
195 Sternitur et quaedam pars duro umbone virorum.

Waltharius tamen in medio furit agmine bello,
Obvia quaeque metens armis ac limite pergens.
Hunc ubi conspiciunt hostes tantas dare strages,
Ac si praesentem metuebant cernere mortem,
200 Et quemcunque locum, seu dextram sive sinistram,
Waltharius peteret, cuncti mox terga dederunt
Et versis scutis laxisque feruntur habenis.

Tunc imitata ducem gens maxima Pannoniarum
205 Saevior insurgit caedemque audacior auget,
Deicit obstantes, fugientes proterit usque,
Dum caperet plenum belli sub sorte triumphum.
Tum super occisos ruit et spoliaverat omnes.
Et tandem ductor recavo vocat agmina cornu
Ac primus frontem festa cum fronde revinxit,
210 Victrici lauro cingens sua timpora vulgo,
Post hunc signiferi, sequitur quos cetera pubes.
Iamque triumphali redierunt stemmate compti
Et patriam ingressi propria se quisque locavit
Sede, sed ad solium mox Waltharius properavit.

215 Ecce palatini decurrunt arce ministri
Illius aspectu hilares equitemque tenebant,
Donec vir sella descenderet inclitus alta.
Si bene res vergant, tum demum forte requirunt.

lances swung through the air and flashed like lightning,
then, thick as snow whipped up by northern gales
in winter-time, the sharp arrows rose and fell.
At last, when every spear on both sides had been hurled,
each hand reached down and grasped its fighting-sword.
Blades flashed like lightning, shields were raised,
the battle lines moved up, and close combat began.
Horses were killed in the press of body against body,
and men felled all around from shield-boss blows.

Walthari, always in the thick of battle, stormed
and hacked a path through anything that stood
against him. When the enemy saw this blood-bath
they believed that they were seeing Death incarnate,
and everywhere that Walthari fought, this way or that,
the enemy soon showed him their heels in flight,
with reins slack and their shields across their backs.

The mighty Huns fought just like their general,
rushed in more fiercely, were bolder in the attack
hacked down those who resisted, trampled those who fled,
until the lottery of war gave them the victory.
They fell upon the dead and stripped them of their gear,
and then their general blew his horn to call his troops,
and donned himself the laurel-crown of victory
before all his men. The standard-bearers followed suit
and every one of the young warriors did the same.
Then, bearing the badge of triumph, they returned,
and having reached their homeland, each man sought
his own home. But Walthari hurried to the court.

Look! How all the palace servants rush about
delighted to see him, rushing to hold the horse
when the great warrior dismounts from his high saddle.
And then they want to know if things went well.

Ille aliquid modicum narrans intraverat aulam,
220 lassus enim fuerat), regisque cubile petebat.
Illic Hiltgundem solam offendit residentem.
Cui post amplexus atque oscula dulcia dixit:
'ocius huc potum ferto, quia fessus anhelo.'
Illa mero tallum complevit mox pretiosum
225 Porrexitque viro, qui signans accipiebat
Virgineamque manum propria constrinxit. at illa
Astitit et vultum reticens intendit herilem,
Walthariusque bibens vacuum vas porrigit olli
Ambo etenim norant de se sponsalia facta—
230 Provocat et tali caram sermone puellam:
'Exilium pariter patimur iam tempore tanto,
Non ignorantes, quid nostri forte parentes
Inter se nostra de re fecere futura.
Quamne diu tacito premimus haec ipsa palato?'
235 Virgo per hyroniam meditans hoc dicere sponsum
Paulum conticuit, sed postea talia reddit:
'Quid lingua simulas, quod ab imo pectore damnas,
Oreque persuades, toto quod corde refutas,
Sit veluti talem pudor ingens ducere nuptam?"
240 Vir sapiens contra respondit et intulit ista:
'absit quod memoras! dextrorsum porrige sensum!
Noris me nihilum simulata mente locutum
Nec quicquam nebulae vel falsi interfore crede.
Nullus adest nobis exceptis namque duobus:
245 Si nossem temet mihi promptam impendere mentem
Atque fidem votis servare per omnia cautis,
Pandere cuncta tibi cordis mysteria vellem.'

Tandem virgo viri genibus curvata profatur:
'ad quaecumque vocas, mi domne, sequar studiose
250 Nec quicquam placitis malim praeponere iussis.'
Ille dehinc: 'piget exilii me denique nostri
Et patriae fines reminiscor saepe relictos

TRANSLATION

Giving a quick account, he entered the great hall, went
—tired as he was—straight for the royal chambers,
and there found Hildigunda, waiting alone.
He took her in his arms and kissed her.
Then he said: "Bring me something to drink! I am exhausted!"
Quickly she filled a jewelled cup with wine
and gave it to the warrior. He took it, crossed himself,
and then he took the maiden's hand in his. The girl
stood silent, looking deep into his face,
while Walthari drained the wine-cup at a draught
—both of them mindful and aware of their betrothal*—
and then said to the girl he loved so dearly:
"We both have had to endure exile so long,
knowing full well what our parents had planned
between themselves for our futures and our lives.
For how much longer must we remain silent?"
The maiden thought her lover's words were ironic,
and did not speak at first. But then she said to him:
"Why do your lips say things you do not really feel?
Your tongue speaks words that are not in your heart!
Would it mean great disgrace to take such a bride?"
But Walthari, wiser, interrupted her and said:
"Not so, not so! Do not misunderstand my words!
Know this: I never have pretended, covered up
false declarations with some smoke-screen of a lie!
No one is here except us two. If I were sure
that your mind were as one with mine,
and you would follow me faithfully in all my plans,
then I would show you every secret in my heart."

The girl knelt at the warrior's feet and said to him:
"My lord, I'll follow you in all that you command.
Nothing shall stop me; I shall do what you wish."
He answered: "This exile we share is hateful to me,
memories of homeland are always in my mind,

Idcircoque fugam cupio celerare latentem.
Quod iam prae multis potuissem forte diebus,
255 Si non Hiltgundem solam remanere dolerem.'
Addidit has imo virguncula corde loquelas:
'Vestrum velle meum, solis his aestuo rebus.
Praecipiat dominus, seu prospera sive sinistra
Eius amore pati toto sum pectore praesto.'
260 Waltharius tandem sic virginis inquit in aurem:
'Publica custodem rebus te nempe potestas
Fecerat, idcirco memor haec mea verba notato:
Primis galeam regis tunicamque, trilicem
Assero loricam fabrorum insigne ferentem,
265 Diripe, bina dehinc mediocria scrinia tolle.
His armillarum tantum da Pannonicarum,
Donec vix unum releves ad pectoris imum.
de quater binum mihi fac de more coturnum,
Tantundemque tibi patrans imponito vasis:
270 Sic fors ad summum complentur scrinia labrum.
super a fabris hamos clam posce retortos:
Nostra viatica sint pisces simul atque volucres,
Ipse ego piscator, sed et auceps esse coartor.
Haec intra ebdomadam caute per singula comple.
275 Audistis, quid habere vianti forte necesse est.
Nunc quo more fugam valeamus inire, recludo:
Postquam septenos Phoebus remeaverit orbes,
Regi ac reginae satrapis ducibus famulisque
Sumptu permagno convivia laeta parabo
280 Atque omni ingenio potu sepelire studebo,
Donec nullus erit, qui sentiat hoc, quod agendum est.
Tu tamen interea mediocriter utere vino
Atque sitim vix ad mensam restinguere cura.
Cum reliqui surgant, ad opuscula nota recurre.
285 Ast ubi iam cunctos superat violentia potus,
Tum simul occiduas properemus quaerere partes.'
Virgo memor praecepta viri complevit. et ecce

and I want to escape—in secrecy and in haste.
I could have done so, many days ago, had not
the thought of Hildigunda, left alone, caused me pain."
The maiden's words to him came from her very heart:
"Your will is mine and it is all that I desire.
Tell me, my lord, what I should do. If good or ill,
I can take anything for the love here in my breast."
Lowering his voice, Walthari whispered to the girl:
"You have been given charge of the royal coffers;
now listen well to what I have to say:
first, take the king's helmet and his three-layered coat,
I mean the ringmail tunic with the mark of the smiths.*
Then take two coffers—neither must be too large—
and fill them with arm-rings* of Hunnish gold, until
you can barely lift the coffers up breast-high.
Procure for me four sets of footwear that will fit,
and then the same for you, and put them in the chests,
and this should fill then up completely. Secretly
get well-turned fish-hooks from the smith—we shall
want fish and birds for food when we are on our way,
and I shall be both fisherman and bird-trapper.
Do all these things within the week, but cautiously—
you know now all the things we need for our escape.
Now let me tell you how we shall begin our flight.
When the sun has crossed the heavens seven times,
for the king and queen, their vassals, lords and court
I shall prepare and give a great and splendid feast,
and make sure that they all end in a drunken sleep,
till not a single one sees what is happening.
But you must only take a small amount of wine,
at table, do no more than merely quench your thirst.
When the others rise, then go about your tasks.
When the force of drink has conquered everyone,
then we shall set off westwards with all speed."
The maiden heard and did all he had asked. And then

Praefinita dies epularum venit, et ipse
Waltharius magnis instruxit sumptibus escas.
290 Luxuria in media residebat denique mensa,
Ingrediturque aulam velis rex undique septam.
Heros magnanimus solito quem more salutans
Duxerat ad solium, quod bissus compsit et ostrum.
Consedit laterique duces hinc indeque binos
295 Assedisse iubet; reliquos locat ipse minister.
Centenos simul accubitus iniere sodales,
Diversasque dapes libans conviva resudat.
His et sublatis aliae referuntur edendae,
Atque exquisitum fervebat migma per aurum
300 Aurea bissina tantum stant gausape vasa—
Et pigmentatus crateres Bachus adornat.
Illicit ad haustum species dulcedoque potus.
Waltharius cunctos ad vinum hortatur et escam.

Postquam epulis depulsa fames sublataque mensa,
305 Heros iam dictus dominum laetanter adorsus
Inquit: 'in hoc, rogito, clarescat gratia vestra,
Ut vos inprimis, reliquos tunc laetificetis.'
Et simul in verbo nappam dedit arte peractam
Ordine sculpturae referentem gesta priorum,
310 Quam rex accipiens haustu vacuaverat uno,
Confestimque iubet reliquos imitarier omnes.
Ocius accurrunt pincernae moxque recurrunt,
Pocula plena dabant et inania suscipiebant.
Hospitis ac regis certant hortatibus omnes.
315 Ebrietas fervens tota dominatur in aula,
Balbutit madido facundia fusa palato,
Heroas validos plantis titubare videres.
Taliter in seram produxit bachica noctem
Munera Waltharius retrahitque redire volentes,
320 Donec vi potus pressi somnoque gravati
Passim porticibus sternuntur humotenus omnes.

TRANSLATION

the day arrived for which the feast was planned. Walthari
had prepared a mighty feast of food and drink
and luxury itself presided at his table.
When the king came into the tapestry-hung hall,
the hero welcomed him with customary grace,
and led to him to a throne decked out with purple cloth.
Attila took his seal, and placed two noblemen
at right and left. A chamberlain arranged the rest
at table. A hundred guests were seated at that feast,
and ate dish after dish, and drank until they sweated.
One course was finished and another took its place,
as wonderful food steamed in its golden vessels
—for only gold appeared upon the linen cloth—
while Bacchus, god of wine, adorned the goblets
with sweet drinks that would tempt the taste of everyone.
Walthari urged them all to eat and drink their fill.

The meal was over: now they left the table,
and the warrior said, laughing, to the king,
"with this, my lord, I beg, show us your favor,
let first yourself, and then the others take their ease."
And as he spoke he handed him a decorated cup
engraved with pictures of his ancestors' great deeds.
Attila took it and drained it at one draught,
and gave the order that the rest keep up with him.
The stewards came and went, and came, and served the wine,
brought brimming goblets and took empty ones away.
Attila and their host urged everybody on,
and very soon the whole hall was roaring drunk
and inebriate babbling came from every mouth.
Great heroes—what a sight!—staggered on their feet.
Walthari, far into the night, kept bringing in
Bacchus' best, dissuading anyone who tried to leave,
until the power of drink and sleep overcame them all,
and there they lay, in doorways and in aisles.

Et licet ignicremis vellet dare moenia flammis,
Nullus, qui causam potuisset scire, remansit.

Tandem dilectam vocat ad semet mulierem,
325 Praecipiens causas citius deferre paratas.
Ipseque de stabulis victorem duxit equorum,
Ob virtutem quem vocitaverat ille Leonem.
Stat sonipes ac frena ferox spumantia mandit.
Hunc postquam faleris solito circumdedit, ecce
330 Scrinia plena gazae lateri suspendit utrique.
Atque iteri longo modicella cibaria ponit
Loraque virgineae mandat fluitantia dextrae.
Ipseque lorica vestitus more gigantis
Imposuit capiti rubras cum casside cristas
335 Ingentesque ocreis suras complectitur aureis
Et laevum femur ancipiti praecinxerat ense
Atque alio dextrum pro ritu Pannoniarum:
Is tamen ex una tantum dat vulnera parte.
Tunc hastam dextra rapiens clipeumque sinistra
340 Coeperat invisa trepidus decedere terra.
Femina duxit equum nonnulla talenta gerentem,
In manibusque simul virgam tenet ipsa colurnam,
In qua piscator hamum transponit in undam,
Ut cupiens pastum piscis deglutiat hamum.
345 Namque gravatus erat vir maximus undique telis
Suspectamque habuit cuncto sibi tempore pugnam.
Omni nocte quidem properabant currere, sed cum
Prima rubens terris ostendit lumina Phoebus,
In silvis latitare student et opaca requirunt,
350 Sollicitatque metus vel per loca tuta fatigans.
In tantumque timor muliebria pectora pulsat,
Horreat ut cunctos aurae ventique susurros,
Formidans volucres collisos sive racemos.
Hinc odium exilii patriaeque amor incubat inde.
355 Vicis diffugiunt, speciosa novalia linquunt,

TRANSLATION

Even if he had he set fire to those walls,
there was not one who would have been aware of it.

At last he called the lovely girl to come to him,
told her to bring the things that she had ready.
Meanwhile he led his battle-charger from the stable,
a horse that he called Lion* for its kingly strength—
and there it stood, stamping, and chafing at the bit.
Walthari saddled him up in customary manner, then
he hung the boxes, full of gold, on either side.
He added food, too, for the journey would be long,
then put the loose rein into Hildigunda's hand.
He, dressed in his mailcoat, mighty as a giant,*
put on a helmet with a crest of fiery red,
and strapped leg-armor, made of gold, to his great thighs.
A two-edged sword he buckled on at his left side,
and at his right another, in the fashion of the Huns,*
though this time one that wounds with one edge only.
Grasping a spear in his right hand, a shield in his left
he set out quickly, leaving the hated land.
The maiden led the horse with its great load,
and in her hand she had a hazel-rod, that fishers
use to cast their hooks far out into the waves,
so that the fish, eager for food, take hook and bait.
The mighty warrior, weighed down with his weapons,
was constantly prepared to fight off an attack.
They made what speed they could throughout the night. But when
the Sun-God* showed his first rays, reddening the land
they looked for cover in the darkness of a wood,
and rested—wary, even though the place was safe.
So full of fear was the girl in heart and mind
that she would start at the noise of a rushing wind,
scared by the noise of birds or a cracking twig.
But hate of exile and the love of home gave courage.
They kept away from villages and open fields,

Montibus intonsis cursus ambage recurvos
Sectantes tremulos variant per devia gressus.

Ast urbis populus somno vinoque solutus
Ad medium lucis siluit recubando sequentis.
360 Sed postquam surgunt, ductorem quique requirunt,
Ut grates faciant ac festa laude salutent.
Attila nempe manu caput amplexatus utraque
Egreditur thalamo rex Walthariumque dolendo
Advocat, ut proprium quereretur forte dolorem.
365 Respondent ipsi se non potuisse ministri
Invenisse virum, sed princeps sperat eundem
Hactenus in somno tentum recubare quietum
Occultumque locum sibi delegisse sopori.

Ospirin Hiltgundem postquam cognovit abesse
370 Nec iuxta morem vestes deferre suetum,
Tristior immensis satrapae clamoribus inquit:
'O detestendas, quas heri sumpsimus, escas!
O vinum, quod Pannonias destruxerat omnes!
Quod domino regi iam dudum praescia dixi,
375 Approbat iste dies, quem nos superare nequimus.
En hodie imperii vestri cecidisse columna
Noscitur, en robur procul ivit et inclita virtus:
Waltharius lux Pannoniae discesserat inde,
Hiltgundem quoque mi caram deduxit alumnam.'

380 Iam princeps nimia succenditur efferus ira,
Mutant laetitiam maerentia corda priorem.
Ex humeris trabeam discindit ad infima totam
Et nunc huc animum tristem, nunc dividit illuc.
Ac velut Aeolicis turbatur arena procellis,
385 Sic intestinis rex fluctuat undique curis,
Et varium pectus vario simul ore imitatus,
Prodidit exterius, quicquid toleraverat intus,

took winding paths instead, on wooded mountain-sides,
and fearful as they were, followed half-hidden tracks.

The people of Attila's court, in sleep and wine
stayed where they lay until the following noon,
but once awake, they tried to find their general,
to thank him for the feast, and offer him their praise.
Attila, with his aching head held in his hands,
came from his chamber, and in wretchedness called for
Walthari, so he could bemoan his sufferings.
His servants said that Walthari was nowhere to
be seen. The king, however, still assumed that he
would be in some dark, hidden nook that he had found
for himself, still sunk in a sound unhearing sleep.

Then Ospirina noticed Hildigunda's absence.
Unusually, she failed to bring the queen her clothes.
The stricken Ospirina cried out to the king:
"A thousand curses on our feasting yesterday
and on the wine, the downfall of all the Huns!
What I foresaw and had already told the king
has now come true, and we shall not get over it.
The mainstay of your empire has given way today,
its power, support, and all its famous strength has gone,
Walthari, the jewel of the Huns, has fled,
and taken my dear and favored Hildigunda."

And now the king* himself flared up in fearful rage,
as all his happiness gave way to heartache.
He tore his robe from his shoulders and threw it down,
his anguished mind filled with conflicting thoughts.
Just as the east wind churns up and drives the sands,
so was the king's mood, with wave on wave of sorrow,
his inner feelings turned this way and that, and what
went on inside him was reflected in his face,

Iraque sermonem permisit promere nullum.
Ipso quippe die potum fastidit et escam,
390 Nec placidam membris potuit dare cura quietem.
Namque ubi nox rebus iam dempserat atra colores,
Decidit in lectum, verus nec lumina clausit,
Nunc latus in dextrum fultus nunc inque sinistrum,
Et veluti iaculo pectus transfixus acuto
395 Palpitat atque caput huc et mox iactitat illuc,
Et modo subrectus fulcro consederat amens.
Nec iuvat hoc, demum surgens discurro in urbe,
Atque thorum veniens simul attigit atque reliquit.
Taliter insomnem consumpserat Attila noctem.

400 At profugi comites per amica silentia euntes
Suspectam properant post terga relinquere terram.

Vix tamen erupit cras, rex patribusque vocatis
Dixerat: 'o si quis mihi Waltharium fugientem
Afferat evinctum ceu nequam forte liciscam!
405 Hunc ego mox auro vestirem saepe recocto
Et tellure quidem stantem hinc inde onerarem
Atque viam penitus clausissem vivo talentis.'

Sed nullus fuit in tanta regione tyrannus
Vel dux sive comes seu miles sive minister,
410 Qui, quamvis cuperet proprias ostendere vires
Ac virtute sua laudem captare perennem
Ambiretque simul gazam infarcire cruminis,
Waltharium tamen iratum praesumpserit armis
Insequier strictoque virum mucrone videre.
415 Nota equidem virtus, experti sunt quoque, quantas
Incolumis dederit strages sine vulnere victor.

Nec potis est ullum rex persuadere virorum,
Qui promissa velit hac condicione talenta.

although his anger would not let him say a word.
That whole day he would neither eat nor drink at all,
and his sorrows allowed his troubled mind no rest.
Night came, obscuring all the colors of the day,
the king fell on his bed, but never closed an eye,
tossing from side to side and from right to left,
feeling as if a spear had cut into his breast.
He started up, and tossed his head this way and that,
then sat bolt upright on his bed, a man distraught.
No help for it! He moved about within his fortress,
came back to bed, and then at once got up again,
and in that way he passed a long and sleepless night.

Meanwhile the fleeing lovers hurried on, through
friendly silence, leaving the hated land behind.

Next day had barely dawned when Attila called in
his counsellors, and said: "If anyone can bring
the fugitive Walthari, like a greyhound bitch
in chains, I'll cover that man with pure gold
from every side when he stands before me, and as
I live,* I'll spread treasures on every path he treads."

But there was no great warlord in all those lands,
no earl, no margrave, no baron and no knight
prepared, however much he wished to show his strength
and gain eternal glory for his bravery
(and fill his coffers with the rich rewards as well),
to try his hand against the anger of Walthari
and meet him face to face with a sword in his hand.
Walthari's strength was known, and all men knew too well
how many blows he gave, to win without a wound.

The king could not persuade a single warrior
to try for the rewards against odds like these.

Waltharius fugiens, ut dixi, noctibus ivit,
420 Atque die saltus arbustaque densa requirens
Arte accersitas pariter capit arte volucres,
Nunc fallens visco, nunc fisso denique ligno.
Ast ubi pervenit, qua flumina curva fluebant,
Immittens hamum rapuit sub gurgite praedam.
425 Atque famis pestem pepulit tolerando laborem.

Namque fugae toto se tempore virginis usu
Continuit vir Waltharius laudabilis heros.

Ecce quater denos sol circumflexerat orbes,
Ex quo Pannonica fuerat digressus ab urbe.
430 Ipso quippe die, numerum qui clauserat istum,
Venerat ad fluvium iam vespere tum mediante,
Scilicet ad Rhenum, qua cursus tendit ad urbem
Nomine Wormatiam regali sede nitentem.
Illic pro naulo pisces dedit antea captos
435 Et mox transpositus graditur properanter anhelus.

Orta dies postquam tenebras discusserat atras,
Portitor exurgens praefatam venit in urbem
Regalique coco, reliquorum quippe magistro,
Detulerat pisces, quos vir dedit ille viator.
440 Hos dum pigmentis condisset et apposuisset
Regi Gunthario, miratus fatur ab alto:
'Istius ergo modi pisces mihi Francia numquam
Ostendit: reor externis a finibus illos.
Dic mihi quantocius: cuias homo detulit illos?'
445 Ipseque respondens narrat, quod nauta dedisset.
Accersire hominem princeps praecepit eundem;
Et, cum venisset, de re quaesitus eadem
Talia dicta dedit causamque ex ordine pandit:
'Vespere praeterito residebam litore Rheni
450 Conspexique viatorem propere venientem

TRANSLATION

Walthari, making his escape, moved on at night,
seeking in daylight gullies and dense thickets,
set lures for birds and caught them skillfully,
sometimes with lime, at others with a split-wood snare.
But if he came to a place where a river meandered,
then he would cast a hook, and haul out his prize.
He worked with a will and thus kept hunger at bay.

And all the time, throughout their flight, Walthari kept
decently* from the girl, just as a warrior should.

Full forty times the sun had risen and had set
since their escape from the fortress of the Huns,
and on that very day, the fortieth of the flight,
at dusk Walthari reached a river, came upon
the Rhine, just where it bends towards the town
of Worms,* a royal capital, the seat of kings.
He paid a ferryman with fish* caught earlier
and, soon across the river, pressed on with all speed.

Next morning, once the day had driven off the dark,
the ferryman got up and set off into the town,
and gave the king's cook (chief of all the rest)
the fishes that the traveller had given him.
The cook prepared them well with herbs, and served them up
to Gundahari, to the king, who said, amazed:
"This kind of fish is unknown in the kingdom
of the Franks. Someone has brought them from another land.
I want to know at once: who sold you fish like this?"
The cook told him that they were from the ferryman,
and Gundahari ordered that the man be fetched.
The man came, and when asked about the matter
gave a full account of everything. He said:
"Yesterday evening I was by the Rhine, and saw
a wanderer who was hurrying towards me,

Et veluti pugnae certum per membra paratum:
Aere etenim penitus fuerat, rex inclite, cinctus
Gesserat et scutum gradiens hastamque coruscam.
Namque viro forti similis fuit, et licet ingens
455 Asportaret onus, gressum tamen extulit acrem.
Hunc incredibili formae decorata nitore
Assequitur calcemque terit iam calce puella.
Ipsaque robustum rexit per lora caballum
Scrinia bina quidem dorso non parva ferentem,
460 Quae, dum cervicem sonipes discusserit altam
Atque superba cupit glomerare volumina crurum,
Dant sonitum, ceu quis gemmis illiserit aurum.
Hic mihi praesentes dederat pro munere pisces.'

His Hagano auditis—ad mensam quippe resedit—
465 Laetior in medium prompsit de pectore verbum:
Congaudete mihi quaeso, quia talia novi:
Waltharius collega meus remeavit ab Hunis.'

Guntharius princeps ex hac ratione superbus
Vociferatur, et omnis ei mox aula reclamat:
470 'Congaudete mihi iubeo, quia talia vixi!
Gazam, quam Gibicho regi transmisit eoo,
Nunc mihi cunctipotens huc in mea regna remisit.'
Haec ait et mensam pede perculit exiliensque
Ducere equum iubet et sella componere sculpta
475 Atque omni de plebe viros secum duodenos
Viribus insignes, animis plerumque probatos
Legerat. inter quos simul ire Haganona iubebat.
Qui memor antiquae fidei sociique prioris
Nititur a coeptis dominum transvertere rebus.
480 Rex tamen econtra nihilominus instat et infit:
'Ne tardate, viri, praecingite corpora ferro
Fortia, squamosus thorax iam terga recondat.
Hic tantum gazae Francis deducat ab oris?'

a man fully armed, clearly prepared for battle.
Lord king, this man was clad in bronze from head to foot!
He strode along, with shield and with a shining spear,
just like a mighty warrior. However much
he carried, still it did not slow him down.
A lady whose beauty was quite beyond belief
was close behind him, following hard at his heels.
She led a mighty battle-charger on a rein,
a horse which carried on its back two massive chests.
When that horse tossed its head and shook its mane,
and, proud beast that it was, paced hard or reared,
there came a sound like jingling gold or jewels.
That warrior gave the fish to me as payment."

Hagano heard this—he was sitting at the table—
and said to all the company in great delight
"Rejoice with me, I beg, at such a piece of news!
My friend Walthari has come back from the Huns."

But Gundahari, proud prince that he was, excited
by this news, cried out, so all the hall resounded:
"Rejoice with me, I say, that I should see such a thing!
The tribute treasure sent to Attila by Gibicho
has been returned to my lands by almighty God."
With that he kicked the table to one side, gave orders
for his horse and finest saddle to be brought, then chose
from all the people there a group of twelve* strong men,
all tested warriors, known for their bravery,
and ordered Hagano to join this group as well.
Thinking of his old loyalty and of his friends,
he tried as best he could to change his overlord's mind.
The king, however, not to be swayed, cried out:
"Men! No delays! Strap on your battle-swords,
and let good ring-mail coats cover your bodies.
Should a man like that escape with Frankish treasure?"*

Instructi telis, nam iussio regis adsurget,
485 Exibant portis, te Waltharium cupientes
Cernere et imbellem lucris fraudare putantes.

Sed tamen omnimodis Hagano prohibere studebat,
At rex infelix coeptis resipiscere non vult.

Interea vir magnanimus de flumine pergens
490 Venerat in saltum iam tum Vosagum vocitatum.
Nam nemus est ingens, spatiosum, lustra ferarum
Plurima habens, suetum canibus resonare tubisque.
Sunt in secessu bini montesque propinqui,
Inter quos licet angustum specus extat amoenum,
495 Non tellure cava factum, sed vertice rupum:
Apta quidem statio latronibus illa cruentis.
Angulus hic virides ac vescas gesserat herbas.

'huc', mox ut vidit iuvenis, 'huc' inquit 'eamus,
His iuvat in castris fessum componere corpus.'
500 Nam postquam fugiens Avarum discesserat oris,
Non aliter somni requiem gustaverat idem
Quam super innixus clipeo; vix clauserat orbes.
Bellica tum demum deponens pondera dixit
Virginis in gremium fusus: 'circumspice caute,
505 Hiltgunt, et nebulam si tolli videris atram,
Attactu blando me surgere commonitato,
Et licet ingentem conspexeris ire catervam,
Ne excutias somno subito, mi cara, caveto,
Nam procul hinc acies potis es transmittere puras.
510 Instanter cunctam circa explora regionem.'
Haec ait atque oculos concluserat ipse nitentes
Iamque diu satis optata fruitur requiete.

Ast ubi Guntharius vestigia pulvere vidit,
Cornipedem rapidum saevis calcaribus urget,

TRANSLATION

Heavily armed—just as their king had commanded—
the warriors rode out in search of you, Walthari,
thinking you unwarlike, easy to cheat of the treasure.

Hagano tried in every way he could to stop them
but the ill-starred king would not call off his enterprise.

Meanwhile, noble Walthari had left the river
and had reached the mountains called the Vosges,*
a huge, far-reaching forest, full of many wild beasts,
and echoing often with the noise of hounds and horns.
Two mountains, close to one other, stand apart, a fine
but very narrow gorge stretching up between them,
a cavern not made of earth, but formed from the peaks,
well suited to be a hideaway for vicious bandits,
though the ground was green, covered with luxurious grass.

"Here," said the warrior when he saw it, "here we shall go,
make camp and in this place stretch out our weary limbs."
For all the time on their flight from the lands of the Huns
Walthari had taken no other form of rest than this:
leaning against his great shield, barely closing his eyes.
So, putting down the burden of his weapons, Walthari laid
his head in his companion's lap, and said: "Keep watch,
and if you see dark dust clouds raised, then, Hildigunda,
wake me with your gentle hand, so I can ready myself,
and even if you see a horde of warriors come towards us,
take care, my dearest, not to jolt me out of sleep.
Your eyes are good, and you can see great distances.
Keep careful look-out always, all around this place."
He finished speaking, and then closed his shining eyes,
to enjoy at last the rest which he so much desired.

Gundahari, however, sees his footprints in the dust
and sharply spurs on his courser in pursuit,

515 Exultansque animis frustra sic fatur ad auras:
'Accelerate, viri, iam nunc capietis euntem,
Numquam hodie effugiet, furata talenta relinquet.'
Inclitus at Hagano contra mox reddidit ista:
'Unum dico tibi, regum fortissime, tantum:
520 Si totiens tu Waltharium pugnasse videres
Atque nova totiens, quotiens ego, caede furentem,
Numquam tam facile spoliandum forte putares.
Vidi Pannonias acies, cum bella cierent
Contra Aquilonares sive Australes regiones:
525 Illic Waltharius propria virtute coruscus
Hostibus invisus, sociis mirandus obibat:
Quisquis ei congressus erat, mox Tartara vidit.
O rex et comites, experto credite, quantus
In clipeum surgat, quo turbine torqueat hastam.'
530 Sed dum Guntharius male sana mente gravatus
Nequaquam flecti posset, castris propriabant.

At procul aspiciens Hiltgunt de vertice montis
Pulvere sublato venientes sensit et ipsum
Waltharium placido tactu vigilare monebat.
535 Qui caput attollens scrutatur, si quis adiret.
Eminus illa refert quandam volitare phalangem.
Ipse oculos tersos somni glaucomate purgans
Paulatim rigidos ferro vestiverat artus
Atque gravem rursus parmam collegit et hastam
540 Et saliens vacuas ferro transverberat auras
Et celer ad pugnam telis prolusit amaram.

Comminus ecce coruscantes mulier videt hastas
Ac stupefacta nimis: 'Hunos hic' inquit 'habemus.'
In terramque cadens effatur talia tristis:
545 'Obsecro, mi senior, gladio mea colla secentur,
Ut, quae non merui pacto thalamo sociari,
Nullius ulterius patiar consortia carnis.'

shouting out exultantly for all to hear:
"Faster, my warriors! and soon we'll catch the wanderer.
He won't escape, and must give up the stolen gold."
But Hagano, bravest of fighters, quickly said:
"Let me say one thing to you, O mighty king:
if you had seen Walthari fight as many times as I,
and watched him hurl himself again into the fray,
you would not think to rob him quite so easily.
I saw the vanguard of the Huns go into battle
against the Northerners or warriors from the South,
and Walthari advanced, aflame with bravery,
the terror of the enemy, the wonder of his friends.
To face him was to be despatched at once to hell.
My king, my nobles, hear me out! I know how firm
his grip is on his shield, how well he hurls his spear."
But Gundahari closed his mind to this, would not
give way. And so they came close to Walthari's camp.

But in the mountains Hildigunda saw them from far off
and knew from the dust-cloud that they were coming.
With gentle touch she woke and warned Walthari,
who raised his head and asked if anyone was there.
She told him that a force of warriors was coming near.
Walthari wiped the veil of sleep from his eyes,
slowly strapped the iron armor on his strong limbs,
and then took up again his heavy shield and lance.
Leaping up, he thrust his spear into the empty air,
practising for the bitter fight that was to come.

At once the girl saw the glint of spears close by,
and cried in terror: "The Huns! These are the Huns!"
She threw herself onto the ground, and begged in tears:
"Lord, I beseech you, take your sword and cut my throat,*
so, if we cannot make the marriage we have planned,
I shall not be forced to share another's bed."

83

Tum iuvenis: 'cruor innocuus me tinxerit?' inquit
Et: 'quo forte modo gladius potis est inimicos
550 Sternere, tam fidae si nunc non parcit amicae?
Absit quod rogitas, mentis depone pavorem.
Qui me de variis eduxit saepe periclis,
Hic valet hic hostes, credo, confundere nostros.'

Haec ait atque oculos tollens effatur ad ipsam:
555 Non assunt Avares hic, sed Franci nebulones,
Cultores regionis,' et en galeam Haganonis
Aspicit et noscens iniunxit talia ridens:
Et meus hic socius Hagano collega veternus.'

Hoc heros dicto introitum stationis adibat,
560 Inferius stanti praedicens sic mulieri:
'Hac coram porta verbum modo iacto superbum:
Hinc nullus rediens uxori dicere Francus
Praesumet se impune gazae quid tollere tantae.'
Necdum sermonem complevit, humotenus ecce
565 Corruit et veniam petiit, quia talia dixit.
Postquam surrexit, contemplans cautius omnes:
'Horum quos video nullum Haganone remoto
Suspicio: namque ille meos per proelia mores
Iam didicit, tenet hic etiam sat callidus artem.
570 Quam si forte volente deo intercepero solam,
Tunc' ait 'ex pugna tibi, Hiltgunt sponsa, reservor.'

Ast ubi Waltharium tali statione receptum
Conspexit Hagano, satrapae mox ista superbo
Suggerit: 'o senior, desiste lacessere bello
575 Hunc hominem! pergant primum, qui cuncta requirant,
Et genus et patriam nomenque locumque relictum,
Vel si forte petat pacem sine sanguine praebens
Thesaurum. per responsum cognoscere homonem
Possumus, et si Waltharius remoratur ibidem,

TRANSLATION

"Shall innocent blood be on my hands?" the warrior said.
Then: "How could my sword cut down the enemy
if it does not spare such a faithful companion?
No more of what you ask! Drive all fear from your mind!
He who has preserved me in perils of all kinds
will put aside our enemies once more—my faith's in Him."

And as he spoke, he raised his eyes, and then he said:
"These are no Huns. These are the Franks, the Nibelungs!*
This land's inhabitants!" And then he saw Hagano's
helmet, recognized it, and said with a laugh:
"My old comrade-in-arms, Hagano is there, too."

When he had spoken, the warrior took up his stance
at the entrance to the gorge, and said to the girl:
"Here at the gateway I declare my defiance!
None of the Franks shall go unharmed to tell his wife
that he took my treasure and lived to tell the tale."
When he had made this vow, he sank down to his knees
and begged forgiveness* of God for saying such a thing.
Then he stood up and looked carefully at all the men.
"Of those I see, not one causes me anxiety
except Hagano, for he alone knows how I fight,
and he himself is skilled in the arts of war.
If by God's grace I can withstand this one in battle,
then I shall return to you, my bride, my Hildigunda."

Now when Hagano saw how Walthari had placed
himself, he quickly said to his arrogant overlord:
"My king, you must not call this man to arms!
First let men go and ask what is his family,
his homeland and his name, and where he has come from.
He may still sue for peace and give the treasure up
without bloodshed. And we shall know the man from his
reply. For if indeed this man is Walthari

580 —Est sapiens—forsan vestro concedet honori.

Praecipit ire virum cognomine rex Camalonem,
Inclita Mettensi quem Francia miserat urbi
Praefectum, qui dona ferens devenerat illo
Anteriore die quam princeps noverit ista.
585 Qui dans frena volat rapidoque simillimus Euro
Transcurro spatium campi iuvenique propinquat
Ac sic obstantem compellat: 'dic, homo, quisnam
Sis. aut unde venis? quo pergere tendis?'
Heros magnanimus respondit talia dicens:
590 'Sponte tua venias an huc te miserit ullus,
Scire velim.' Camalo tunc reddidit ore superbo:
'Noris Guntharium regem tellure potentem
Me misisse tuas quaesitum pergere causas.'

His auscultatis suggesserat hoc adolescens:
595 'Ignoro penitus, quid opus sit forte viantis
Scrutari causas, sed promere non trepidamus.
Waltharius vocor, ex Aquitanis sum generatus.
A genitore meo modicus puer obsidis ergo
Sum datus ad Hunos, ibi vixi nuncque recessi
600 Concupiens patriam dulcemque revisere gentem.'
Missus ad haec: 'tibi iam dictus per me iubet heros,
Ut cum scriniolis equitem des atque puellam:
Quod si promptus agis, vitam concedet et artus.'

Waltharius contra fidenter protulit ista:
605 'Stultius effatum me non audisse sophistam
En memoras, quod princeps nescio vel quis
Promittat, quod non retinet nec fors retinebat.
An deus est, ut iure mihi concedere possit
Vitam? num manibus tetigit? num carcere trusit
610 Vel post terga meas torsit per vincula palmas?
At tamen ausculta: si me certamine laxat

TRANSLATION

—who is no fool—he may give way before your rank."

King Gundahari sent out a man named Kamalo*
who served the great land of the Franks as governor
of Metz. He had arrived with gifts the previous day,
before the king had heard about Walthari.
Kamalo gave his horse its head, and like the very wind
he raced across the plain and came to the young man.
He reached the warrior and demanded: "Tell me who
you are, where you are from and where you wish to go."
The noble warrior Walthari answered him:
"I want to know if you ride for yourself, or as
another's messenger." Kamalo answered haughtily:
"Know this! King Gundahari, highest in the land
sent me, and he demands to know your business."

When he had heard these words, the young warrior said:
"I see no cause why anyone should want to know
about a wanderer. But I am not afraid
to speak. I am Walthari, from the Aquitaine.
When I was young, my father gave me to the Huns
as hostage. There I lived, then longing made me leave
to see my dear land and its people once again."
Kamalo said: "Lord Gundahari orders you through me
to give up the treasure-chests, your horse and the girl,
and if you do so quickly, he will let you live."

Calmly, Walthari made him this reply:
"I think that I have never heard such nonsense from
an educated man. You say some king or other
promises me what is not, cannot be, his to give.
Or is he God, that he presumes to give or take
my life? Has he laid hands on, or imprisoned me?
Or has he manacled my arms behind my back?
Now you hear this! If he spares me a battle,

Aspicio, ferratus adest, ad proelia venit—,
Armillas centum de rubro quippe metallo
Factas transmittam, quo nomen regis honorem.'
615 Tali responso discesserat ille recepto,
Principibus narrat, quod protulit atque resumpsit.

Tunc Hagano ad regem: 'porrectam suscipe gazam,
Hac potis es decorare, pater, tecum comitantes,
Et modo de pugna palmam revocare memento.
620 Ignotus tibi Waltharius et maxima virtus.
Ut mihi praeterita portendit visio nocte,
Non, si conserimus, nos prospera cuncta sequentur.
Visum quippe mihi te colluctarier urso,
Qui post conflictus longos tibi mordicus unum
625 Crus cum poplite ad usque femur decerpserat omne
Et mox auxilio subeuntem ac tela ferentem
Me petit atque oculum cum dentibus eruit unum.'

His animadversis clamat rex ille superbus:
'Ut video, genitorem imitaris Hagathien ipse.
630 Hic quoque perpavidam gelido sub pectore mentem
Gesserat et multis fastidit proelia verbis.'

Tunc heros magnam iuste conceperat iram,
Si tamen in dominum licitum est irascier ullum.
En' ait 'in vestris consistant omnia telis.
635 Est in conspectu, quem vultis. dimicet omnis.
Comminus astatis nec iam timor impedit ullum;
Eventum videam nec consors sim spoliorum.'
Dixerat et collem petiit mox ipse propinquum
Descendensque ab equo consedit et aspicit illo.

640 Post haec Guntharius Camaloni praecipit aiens:
'Perge et thesaurum reddi mihi praecipe totum.
Quodsi cunctetur—scio tu vir fortis et audax—

TRANSLATION

(I see that he is armed and ready for a fight),
then I shall give a hundred arm-rings of red gold
to him, in tribute to the honor of a king."
When he heard this reply, the messenger returned
and told the nobles what he had brought back.

Hagano told the king: "You should accept this treasure.
With it, my Lord, you can reward your followers.
Only be sure to keep your hand from battle!
Walthari and his great strength are unknown to you.
I had a dream* last night, and it was clear to me
that if we fight, then things will not go well with us.
For in my dream I saw you fighting with a bear
which after hours of fighting tore off with its teeth
one of your legs, beyond the knee and to the thigh!
And when I came with weapons to your aid, it went
for me, tore out one of my eyes, knocked out my teeth."

But hearing this, the king in his arrogance cried:
"As I can see, you are like your father, Hagathio,*
whose spirit trembled inside a shivering body,
and who used words to help him to avoid a fight!"

The hero Hagano grew justly angry then
(if anger is ever just against an overlord),
and said: "So be it. Now your weapons must decide.
The man you want stands there before you. Now let all
men fight. You see him, and no terror holds you back.
I'll watch the outcome, and I want none of the spoils."
When he had spoken, he strode to a nearby hill,
dismounted quickly, then sat down to watch the fray.

Then Gundahari ordered Kamalo once more:
"Go back, command that all the treasure come to me.
If he should hesitate—I know that you are brave—

Congredere et bello devictum mox spoliato.'

Ibat Mettensis Camalo metropolitanus,
645 Vertice fulva micat cassis, de pectore thorax,
Et procul acclamans: 'heus! audi' dixit 'amice!
Regi Francorum totum transmitte metallum
Si vis ulterius vitam vel habere salutem!'

Conticuit paulum verbo fortissimus heros,
650 Opperiens propius hostem adventare ferocem.
Advolitans missus vocem repetiverat istam.
'Regi Francorum totum transmitte metallum!'
Tum iuvenis constans responsum protulit istud:
'Quid quaeris? vel quid reddi, importune, coartas?
655 Numquid Gunthario furabar talia regi?
Aut mihi pro lucro quicquam donaverat ille,
Ut merito usuram me cogat solvere tantam?
Num pergens ego damna tuli vestrae regioni,
Ut vel hinc iuste videar spoliarier a te?
660 Si tantam invidiam cunctis gens exhibet ista,
Ut calcare solum nulli concedat eunti,
Ecce viam mercor, regi transmitto ducentas
Armillas. pacem donet modo bella remittens.'

Haec postquam Camalo percepit corde ferino,
665 'Amplificabis' ait 'donum, dum scrinia pandis.
Consummare etenim sermones nunc volo cunctos:
Aut quaesita dabis aut vitam sanguine fundes.'
Sic ait et triplicem clipeum collegit in ulnam
Et crispans hastile micans vi nititur omni
670 Ac iacit. at iuvenis devitat cautior ictum.
Hasta volans casso tellurem vulnere mordit.

Waltharius tandem: 'si sic placet', inquit, 'agamus!'
Et simul in dictis hastam transmisit. at illa

attack, and when you win, strip him of everything."

Kamalo, Governor of Metz, then set out, a helmet
shining golden on his head, his armor on,
and from the distance he cried out: "Hear me, my friend!
Give over all your gold to the King of the Franks
if you would like to keep your life and health!"

Walthari, mightiest of warriors, was silent,
waiting for his grim adversary to come closer.
The messenger came onwards, and said as before:
"Give over all your gold to the King of the Franks!"*
The young warrior stood firm and answered him:
"What is it that you want? What do you ask so rudely
for me to give up? Have I robbed Gundahari
of such things? Or did he make me some kind of loan
which merits forcing me to pay such interest?
In passing through, have I done damage to your lands,
to justify, perhaps, thus being robbed by you?
However, if your nation hates everyone so much
that they will let no traveller go his way,
then let me pay for passage, give the king two hundred
arm-rings. Let him make peace, then, and desist from war."

Kamalo heard this with the fury of an animal,
and said: "You'll give a lot more when those chests are opened!
And now I want to put an end to all these words.
Give me what I have asked, or pay with your life's blood."
With that he settled his thick* shield on his arm
swung out his shining spear and gathered all his strength
to throw. Walthari took care to avoid the blow.
The flying spear bit, gave the earth a futile wound.

Walthari at last said: "Well, so be it! Let us fight,"
and as he did so, hurled his spear at Kamalo. His lance

Per laevum latus umbonis transivit, et ecce
675 Palmam, qua Camalo mucronem educere coepit,
Confixit femori transpungens terga caballi.
Nec mora, dum vulnus sentit sonipes, furit atque
Excutiens dorsum sessorem sternere temptat;
Et forsan faceret, ni lancea fixa teneret.
680 Interea parmam Camalo dimisit et, hastam
Complexus laeva, satagit divellere dextram.
Quod mox perspiciens currit celeberrimus heros
Et pede compresso capulo tenus ingerit ensem;
Quem simul educens hastam de vulnere traxit.
685 Tunc equus et dominus hora cecidere sub una.

Et dum forte nepos conspexerat hoc Camalonis,
Filius ipsius Kimo cognomine fratris,
Quem referunt quidam Scaramundum nomine dictum,
Ingemit et lacrimis compellat tristior omnes:
690 'Haec me prae cunctis heu respicit actio rerum.
Nunc aut commoriar vel carum ulciscar amicum.'
Namque angusta loci solum concurrere soli
Cogebant, nec quisquam alii succurrere quivit.
Advolat infelix Scaramundus iam moriturus,
695 Bina manu lato crispans hastilia ferro.
Qui dum Waltharium nullo terrore videret
Permotum fixumque loco consistere in ipso,
Sic ait infrendens et equinam vertice caudam
Concutiens: 'in quo fidis? vel quae tua spes est?
700 Non ego iam gazam nec rerum quidque tuarum
Appeto, sed vitam cognati quaero perempti.'
Ille dehinc: 'si convincar, quod proelia primus
Temptarim, seu quid merui, quod talia possim
Jure pati, absque mora tua me transverberet hasta.'
705 Necdum sermonem concluserat, en Scaramundus
Unum de binis hastile retorsit in illum
Confestimque aliud. quorum celeberrimus heros

pierced through the left side of his shield. Amazingly*
it pinned the hand, with which Kamalo was about
to draw his sword, to his thigh, and speared his horse.
The battle-charger felt the wound, reared up at once
shaking his back to try and throw the rider off,
and might have done so, had the lance not held them fast.
Meanwhile Kamalo dropped his shield, and having grasped
his spear in his left hand now tried to free his right.
The mighty warrior saw this, and at once he ran
and held his leg* and pushed his sword into his side.
When he withdrew his sword and then pulled back his spear,
then the horse and rider fell at the same time.

Kamalo's nephew,* watching, saw what had happened
—his brother's son, the one who bore the name Kimo,
and who himself was, as we hear, called Skaramund—
and sighed, and through his tears said to the others there:
"The battle now, alas, is mine above all others.
Now let me die too, or else avenge my dear kinsman."
The narrow gorge permitted only single combat,
no one could help one of his fellow warriors.
About to die, unlucky Skaramund moved in
with two broad-headed iron-tipped spears in hand.
When he saw that Walthari never flinched with fear,
but stood firm and unmoving in that place,
he said, gnashing his teeth and shaking his helmet*
with its plumes: "Where is your faith? What hope have you now?
I want no treasure, nor do I seek to take
your goods, but I demand revenge for my kinsman's life."
Walthari said: "If it be proved that I was first
to fight, or that I have deserved to suffer it
in justice, may your spear then pierce me through at once."
Before he finished speaking, Skaramund took one
of his two spears, and threw it at the warrior,
and right away the other. The great Walthari

Unum devitat, quatit ex umbone secundum.
Tunc aciem gladii promens Scaramundus acuti
710 Proruit in iuvenem cupiens praescindere frontem,
Effrenique in equo propius devectus ad illum
Non valuit capiti libratum infindere vulnus,
Sed capulum galeae impegit; dedit illa resultans
Tinnitus ignemque simul transfudit ad auras.
715 Sed non cornipedem potuit girare superbum,
Donec Waltharius sub mentum cuspidis ictum
Fixerat et sella moribundum sustulit alta.
Qui caput orantis proprio mucrone recidens
Fecit cognatum pariter fluitare cruorem.
720 Hunc ubi Guntharius conspexit obisse superbus,
Hortatur socios pugnam renovare furentes:
'Aggrediamur eum nec respirare sinamus,
Donec deficiens lassescat; et inde revinctus
Thesauros reddet luet et pro sanguine poenas.'

725 Tertius en Werinhardus abit bellumque lacessit,
Quamlibet ex longa generatus stirpe nepotum,
O vir clare, tuus cognatus et artis amator,
Pandare, qui quondam iussus confundere foedus
In medios telum torsisti primus Achivos.
730 Hic spernens hastam pharetram gestavit et arcum,
Eminus emissis haud aequo Marte sagittis
Waltharium turbans. contra tamen ille virilis
Constitit opponens clipei septemplicis orbem,
Saepius eludens venientes providus ictus.
735 Nam modo dissiluit, parmam modo vergit in austrum
Telaque discussit, nullum tamen attigit illum.
Postquam Pandarides se consumpsisse sagittas
Incassum videt, iratus mox exerit ensem
Et demum advolitans has iactitat ore loquelas:
740 'O si ventosos lusisti callide iactus,
Forsan vibrantis dextrae iam percipis ictum.'

TRANSLATION

dodged the first, and shook the other from his shield.
Then Skaramund drew the blade of his sharp sword
and came in close, wanting to split his skull in two.
His horse, unreined, brought him too near his enemy,
and he could not swing out to wound Walthari's head.
Instead the pommel hit the helmet,* ringing out
a sound, and at the same time striking sparks.
Skaramund could not rein in and turn his mighty horse,
Walthari caught him with his lance beneath the chin
and lifted the dying man from his high saddle.
He severed the victim's head then with his own sword,
and thus he made the blood of a second kinsman flow.
Now when proud* Gundahari saw that his man had died
he urged his angry comrades to renew the fight:
"Let us attack, give him no time to catch his breath
until he falls in weariness, and when we take him,
we shall have gold and he will pay the price of blood.

Werinhart* was the third to enter the battle,
scion of a long line of warrior ancestors.
This man is kin of yours, with the selfsame battle-skills,
O noble Pandarus, whom the Gods made break the truce
and loose the first arrow into the Argive ranks!
Scorning a spear, he held a quiver and a bow.
To his advantage he fired arrows from far off,
troubling Walthari. But against this the brave man
stood fast and faced it with his sevenfold shield,
careful always to elude or parry every shot.
Sometimes he leapt aside, sometimes he tipped his shield
and warded off the bolt, and none of them touched him.
When Pandarus' kinsman saw that he had used
his arrows all in vain, he drew his sword in anger,
and then rushed forward, shouting aloud as he ran:
"If you made light of my arrows, fast as the wind
perhaps you will feel a blow swung from my right arm!"

95

Olli Waltharius ridenti pectore adorsus:
'Iamque diu satis expecto certamina iusto
Pondere agi. festina, in me mora non erit ulla.'
745 Dixerat et toto conixus corpore ferrum
Conicit. hasta volans pectus reseravit equinum:
Tollit se arrectum quadrupes et calcibus auras
Verberat effundensque equitem cecidit super illum.
Currit iuvenis et ei vi diripit ensem.
750 Casside discussa crines complectitur albos
Multiplicesque preces nectenti dixerat heros:
'Talia non dudum iactabas dicta per auras.'
Haec ait et truncum secta cervice reliquit.
Sed non dementem tria visa cadavera terrent
755 Guntharium: iubet ad mortem properare vicissim.
En a Saxonicis oris Ekivrid generatus
Quartus temptavit bellum, qui pro nece facta
Cuiusdam primatis eo diffugerat exul.
Quem spadix gestabat equus maculis variatus.
760 Hic ubi Waltharium promptum videt esse duello,
'Dic', ait, 'an corpus vegetet tractabile temet
Sive per aerias fallas, maledicte, figuras.
Saltibus assuetus faunus mihi quippe videris.'

Illeque sublato dedit haec responsa cachinno:
765 'Celtica lingua probat te ex illa gente creatum,
Cui natura dedit reliquas ludendo praeire.
At si te propius venientem dextera nostra
Attingat, post Saxonibus memorare valebis,
Te nunc in Vosago fauni fantasma videre.'

770 'Attemptabo quidem, quid sis', Ekivrid ait, ac mox
Ferratam cornum graviter iacit. illa retorto
Emicat amento: quam durus fregerat umbo.

TRANSLATION

Smiling to himself, Walthari answered him:
"I have had a long wait before I could engage
in proper combat. Come on, I want no more delay!"
When he had spoken, he drew all his strength, and threw
his iron spear, which tore the flesh of the other's mount.
The horse reared up, and with its hooves struck out into
the air, pitched off its rider and fell onto him.
Walthari ran and tore away the warrior's sword,
pulled off his helmet, and took him by his fair hair,
and said as Werinhart was pleading for his life:
"Just now you shouted other words into the wind
than these." And left his body headless on the ground.
The sight of three dead men did not frighten the crazed
King Gundahari, who ordered still more to their death.
Now Ekifrid,* a warrior from the Saxon shores
was fourth to fight, a man in exile with the Franks
for killing a certain nobleman at home.
He rode a chestnut, a charger with a white blaze.
When he saw Walthari standing ready for the fight
he said: "Tell me, are you a man of flesh and blood,
or is all this, damn you, some kind of fiendish trick?
You look to me like a wood-demon* in its lair!"

Walthari laughed aloud, and then made this reply:
"Your Celtic tongue* proves that you come from that race
put on this earth to serve as jesters to the rest!
If you dare come in closer, so that my right hand
can touch you, you can go and tell your Saxons then
that this time you really saw a Demon of the Vosges!"

"I shall find out what you really are," said Ekifrid,
and fiercely hurled his iron-tipped wooden lance, which flew
out of the throwing-sling, but shattered on the shield.

Waltharius contra respondit cuspide missa:
'Haec tibi silvanus transponit munera faunus.
775 Aspice, num mage sit telum penetrabile nostrum.'
Lancea taurino contextum tergore lignum
Diffidit ac tunicam scindens pulmone resedit.
Volvitur infelix Ekivrid rivumque cruoris
Evomit: en mortem fugiens incurrit eandem.
780 Cuius equum iuvenis post tergum in gramen abegit.

Tunc a Gunthario clipeum sibi postulat ipsum
Quintus ab inflato Hadawardus pectore lusus.
Qui pergens hastam sociis dimisit habendam,
Audax in solum confisus inaniter ensem.
785 Et dum conspiceret deiecta cadavera totam
Conclusisse viam nec equum transire valere,
Dissiliens parat ire pedes. stetit acer in armis
Waltharius laudatque virum, qui praebuit aequam
Pugnandi sortem. Hadawart tum dixit ad illum:
790 'O versute dolis ac fraudis conscie serpens
Occultare artus squamoso tegmine suetus
Ac veluti coluber girum collectus in unum
Tela tot evitas tenui sine vulneris ictu
Atque venenatas ludis sine more sagittas—
795 Numquid et iste putas astu vitabitur ictus,
Quem propius stantis certo libramine mittit
Dextra manus? neque enim is teli seu vulneris auctor.
Audi consilium, parmam deponito pictam:
Hanc mea sors quaerit, regis quoque sponsio praestat;
800 Nolo quidem laedas, oculis quia complacet istis.
Sin alias, licet et lucem mihi dempseris almam,
Assunt hic plures socii carnisque propinqui,
Qui, quamvis volucrem simules pennasque capessas,
Te tamen immunem numquam patientur abire.'

805 Belliger at contra nil territus intulit ista:

Walthari answered, hurling his spear in return:
"The demon of the woods sends you this wooden* gift—
see if the sharpness of my weapons matches yours!"
The lance split up the shield, the bullhide and the wood,
tore through the mail-coat until it pierced the lung.
Unlucky Ekifrid span round and spewed a stream
of blood. He tried to flee, but ran into his death.
Walthari drove his horse into the field behind him.

A fifth man, Hadawart,* now sought from Gundahari
in arrogance, the chance to win Walthari's shield.
When he rode out, he gave his friends his spear to keep,
trusting, boldy but wrongly, in his sword alone.
When he saw that the corpses which were strewn about
now blocked the path and stopped his horse from coming through,
dismounting, he went in on foot. Walthari stood,
bold and well-armed, and praised the man for offering
an equal fight. But Hadawart cried out to him:
"You crafty and deceitful snake, shifting your shape
to hide your limbs beneath a covering of scales,
you put yourself into a tight serpentine coil
and dodge unscathed each weapon that is hurled your way.
You laugh off even arrows tipped with poison!*
But will you, do you think, avoid the blow that he,
who stands here close before you now, will bring
with his right hand? He hurls no wounding spears or arrows.*
Listen to me! Place on the ground your painted shield
—my share of the booty, promised me by the king—
I do not want it damaged, for it pleases me.
But if by some chance you should rob me of the light,
my fellow-warriors and my kinsmen stand prepared,
and even if you turn into some great winged bird
they still would not permit you to escape."

In warlike mood, Walthari, unafraid, replied:

'De reliquis taceo, clipeum defendere curo.
Pro meritis, mihi crede, bonis sum debitor illi.
Hostibus iste meis se opponere saepe solebat
Et pro vulneribus suscepit vulnera nostris.
810 Quam sit oportunus hodie mihi, cernis, et ipse
Non cum Walthario loquereris forsan, abesset.
Viribus o summis hostem depellere cures,
Dextera, ne rapiat tibi propugnacula muri!
Tu clavum umbonis studeas retinere, sinistra,
815 Atque ebori digitos circumfer glutine fixos!
Istic ne ponas pondus, quod tanta viarum
Portasti spatia, ex Avarum nam sedibus altis!'

Ille dehinc: 'invitus agis, si sponte recusas.
Solum parmam, sed equum cum virgine et auro
820 Reddes: tum demum scelerum cruciamina pendes.'
Haec ait et notum vagina diripit ensem.
Inter se variis terrarum partibus orti
Concurrunt. stupuit Vosegus haec fulmina et ictus.
Olli sublimes animis ac grandibus armis,
825 Hic gladio fidens, hic acer et arduus hasta,
Inter se multa et valida vi proelia miscent.
Non sic nigra sonat percussa securibus ilex,
Ut dant tinnitus galeae clipeique resultant.
Mirantur Franci, quod non lassesceret heros
830 Waltharius, cui nulla quies spatiumve dabatur.
Emicat hic impune putans iam Wormatiensis
Alte et sublato consurgit fervidus ense,
Hoc ictu memorans semet finire duellum.
Providus at iuvenis ferientem cuspide adacta
835 Intercepit et ignarum dimittere ferrum
Cogebat. procul in dumis resplenduit ensis.
Hic ubi se gladio spoliatum vidit amico,
Accelerare fugam fruticesque volebat adire.
Alpharides fretus pedibus viridique iuventa

TRANSLATION

"Your other points I ignore. My shield, I shall defend;
to its great virtues I am, believe me, much in debt.
Often it has stood bravely against my enemies,
and has received the wounds that might well have been mine.
You see how useful it has been to me today.
Without it, you would not speak with Walthari now.
May my right hand with all its strength drive off the foe,
lest he should steal you from me, my defense in war!
And let my left hand hold fast to the shield-grip,
my fingers fixed, as if glued to the ivory!
Do not lay down the burden now that you have borne
so very far, right from the city of the Huns!"

Hadawart said: "By force then, if not by free will!
Nor just your shield, but horse and girl and gold as well
you will give up; that way you will pay for your crimes."
With that he drew his noble sword out of its sheath.
The two men—hailing from different lands—rushed against
each other. The mountains marvelled at the thundering blows.
Both men bold, and both armed with the strongest weapons,
one trusting his sword, his keen adversary the lance,
they settled in to fight with every scrap of strength.
The sound of axes struck against a great black oak
is less than that which echoed here from helmets and shields.
The Franks watched in amazement as Walthari fought
without tiring, since no respite was given him.
Hadawart of Worms then thought he had his chance,
and came in rashly with his sword held back and high,
believing he could end the duel with this blow.
But Walthari was wary, thrust his iron spear
to intercept, and took him by surprise. He dropped
his sword, which gleamed a way off in the undergrowth.
Now that he saw himself without his trusty sword,
Hadawart tried to run for cover, to take flight.
Alphari's son,* confident in his youth and speed,

840 Insequitur dicens: 'quonam fugis? accipe scutum!'
Sic ait atque hastam manibus levat ocius ambis
Et ferit. ille cadit, clipeus superintonat ingens.
Nec tardat iuvenis: pede collum pressit et hasta
Divellens parmam telluri infixerat illum.
845 Ipse oculos vertens animam sufflavit in auram.

Sextus erat Patavrid. soror hunc germana Haganonis
Protulit ad lucem. quem dum procedere vidit,
Vocibus et precibus conatur avunculus inde
Flectere proclamans: 'quonam ruis? aspice mortem,
850 Qualiter arridet! desiste! en ultima Parcae
Fila legunt. o care nepos, te mens tua fallit.
Desine! Waltharii tu denique viribus impar.'

Infelix tamen ille means haec omnia sprevit,
Arsit enim venis laudem captare cupiscens.

855 Tristatusque Hagano suspiria pectore longa
Traxit et has imo fudit de corde loquelas:
'O vortex mundi, fames insatiatus habendi,
Gurges avaritiae, cunctorum fibra malorum!
O utinam solum gluttires dira metallum
860 Divitiasque alias, homines impune remittens!
Sed tu nunc homines perverso numine perflans
Incendis nullique suum iam sufficit. ecce
Non trepidant mortem pro lucro incurrere turpem.
Quanto plus retinent, tanto sitis ardet habendi.
865 Externis modo vi modo furtive potiuntur
Et, quod plus renovat gemitus lacrimasque ciebit,
Caeligenas animas Erebi fornace retrudunt.
Ecce ego dilectum nequeo revocare nepotem,
Instimulatus enim de te est, o saeva cupido.
870 En caecus mortem properat gustare nefandam
Et vili pro laude cupit descendere ad umbras.

pursued him with a shout: "Why flee? Here is my shield!"
And as he spoke, he raised his spear with both his hands
and struck. Hadawart fell, the shield on top of him.
Walthari put his foot upon his neck, then pushed
aside the shield and speared Hadawart to the ground.
His eyes rolled up, and thus he breathed his last.

Patafrid* was the sixth. Hagano's own sister
had borne him. When his uncle saw him moving out
to fight, he tried with words and prayers to hold him back,
and shouted: "Wait! Where are you rushing to? Look! Death
is grinning at you! Hold! The Fates are spinning out
your life's last threads. Dear nephew, do not be deceived!
Stay back! You are no match for Walthari's great strength!"

But the ill-fated warrior scorned all this, and went
out, burning with a hot desire to win acclaim.

Hagano, in his sadness, gave out long sighs
and from the very depths of his heart said these words:
"O whirlpool of the world! Insatiable greed!
You maelstrom, avarice, root of every evil!
If only you would swallow up the gold alone,
or that and the other riches, but leave the men!
No, you with your perverseness set men all aflame,
so none remains content with what he has. And look!
When spoils beckon, they do not fear ugly death.
The more they have, the more they lust and burn to get!
By stealth or by force they will take another's goods!
But what renews my sorrow and brings forth hot tears
is that their heaven-born souls will be consigned to hell.
I cannot call my own beloved nephew back,
now that he is beneath your spell, O cruel greed!
See how he rushes blindly into dismal death,
seeking, because of empty fame, the shadowlands.

Heu, mihi care nepos, quid matri, perdite, mandas?
Quis nuper ductam refovebit, care, maritam,
Cui nec, rapte spei, pueri ludicra dedisti?
875 Quis tibi nam furor est? unde haec dementia venit?'

Sic ait et gremium lacrimis conspersit obortis,
Et longum 'formose, vale' singultibus edit.

Waltharius, licet alonge, socium fore maestum
Attendit, clamorque simul pervenit ad aures.
880 Unde incursantem sic est affatus equestrem:
'Accipe consilium, iuvenis clarissime, nostrum
Et te conservans melioribus utere fatis.
Desine, nam tua te fervens fiducia fallit!
Heroum tot cerne neces et cede duello,
885 Ne suprema videns hostes facias mihi plures.'
'Quid de morte mea curas,' ait ille, 'tyranne?
Est modo pugnandum tibimet, non sermocinandum.'
Dixit et in verbo nodosam destinat hastam,
Cuspide quam propria divertens transtulit heros.
890 Quae subvecta choris ac viribus acta furentis
In castrum venit atque pedes stetit ante puellae.
Ipsa metu perculsa sonum prompsit muliebrem.
At postquam tenuis redit in praecordia sanguis,
Paulum suspiciens spectat, num viveret heros.

895 Tum quoque vir fortis Francum discedere bello
Iussit. at ille furens gladium nudavit et ipsum
Incurrens petiit vulnusque a vertice librat.
Alpharides parmam demum concusserat aptam
Et spumantis apri frendens de more tacebat.
900 Ille ferire volens se pronior omnis ad ictum
Exposuit, sed Waltharius sub tegmine flexus
Delituit corpusque suum contraxit, et ecce
Vulnere delusus iuvenis recidebat ineptus.

TRANSLATION

Alas, my dear doomed nephew, what am I to tell
your mother? Who will tend your newly-wedded bride?
She got no son from you, and now she has no hope.
What fury has possessed you? What madness is this?"

Hagano had spoken. Hot tears fell into his lap—
he sobbed long, and said: "Farewell, handsomest of young men."

Walthari, though far off, could see his old friend's
sadness, and he also heard the noise of weeping.
When the rider came to the attack, he said:
"Take my advice, most noble of young warriors,
and spare yourself for a fate better than this.
Hold off! Your fervent confidence leads you astray.
Look at all these already killed, give up your fight,
or you will die, and make more enemies for me!"
"Why should you care about my death, you slaughterer!*
I should be fighting you, and not exchanging words!"
With that, and as he spoke, he hurled his rugged* lance,
which Walthari deflected, striking with his own.
The spear flew, carried by the winds and by Walthari's
force, into their camp and struck by Hildigunda's feet.
She, terrified by this, screamed out, as women do,
but when her heartbeat* ceased to race and pound, she looked
out cautiously, to see if Walthari was still alive.

Again the mighty warrior told the Frank to quit
the fight. But Patafrid in fury took his sword
and rushed to try and wound Walthari from above.
Alphari's son, now silent, swung into place his shield
and like some foam-flecked boar he ground his teeth.
The other hurled his whole self into the attack,*
but Walthari took cover behind his shield,
making himself smaller. The young man, Patafrid,
clumsily missed his blow and fell to the ground.

Finis erat, nisi quod genibus tellure refixis
905 Belliger accubuit calibemque sub orbe cavebat.
Hic dum consurgit, pariter se subrigit ille
Ac citius scutum trepidus sibi praetulit atque
Frustra certamen renovare parabat. at illum
Alpharides fixa gladio petit ocius hasta
910 Et mediam clipei dempsit vasto impete partem,
Hamatam resecans loricam atque ilia nudans.
Labitur infelix Patavrid sua viscera cernens
Silvestrique ferae corpus, animam dedit Orco.

Hunc sese ulturum spondens Gerwitus adivit,
915 Qui forti subvectus equo supra volat omnem
Stragem, quae angustam concluserat obvia callem.
Et dum bellipotens recidisset colla iacentis,
Venit et ancipitem vibravit in ora bipennem.
Istius ergo modi Francis tunc arma fuere.)
920 Vir celer obiecit peltam frustravit et ictum,
Ac retro saliens hastam rapiebat amicam
Sanguineumque ulva viridi dimiserat ensem.

Hic vero metuenda virum tum bella videres.
Sermo quidem nullus fuit inter Martia tela:
925 Sic erat adverso mens horum intenta duello.
Is furit, ut caesos mundet vindicta sodales,
Ille studet vitam toto defendere nisu
Et, si fors dederit, palmam retinere triumphi.
Hic ferit, ille cavet, petit ille, reflectitur iste:
930 Ad studium fors et virtus miscentur in unum
Longa tamen cuspis breviori depulit hostem
Armatum telo, girat sed et ille caballum
Atque fatigatum cupiebat fallere homonem.

Iam magis atque magis irarum mole gravatus
935 Waltharius clipeum Gerwiti sustulit imum,

TRANSLATION

The end was close, but the warrior, on his knees upon
the ground, hid from Walthari's sword behind his shield.
His adversary got up as he gained his feet,
and, frightened now, he took his shield and tried in vain
to start the fight once more. Alphari's son then struck
his spear into the ground, and went in with his sword
with such force that he cut the other's shield half through,
slashed through the chain mail and into the other's chest.
Ill-starred Patafrid saw his entrails spilling out,
and Hades had his soul, the forest-beasts his corpse.

Bent on avenging him, Gerwit* now made his move
and on his strong horse leapt across the many dead,
who now blocked off the narrow entrance-passageway,
and, as the warrior hacked off the dead man's head,
he came and swung his doubled-headed battle-axe—
the Franks once used such weapons—at Walthari's head.
Swiftly he raised his shield and warded off the blow,
and jumping backwards snatched up his old friend, his spear,
and threw his bloody sword down onto the green grass.

Here you could truly see men in a fearsome fight.
No words now, just the weapons of the God of War,
each man with all his mind intent upon combat!
One fights in fury to avenge his dead fellows,
the other seeks with all force to save his life
and keep the palm of victory—if Fate allows.
A strike, a parry, an attack and a repulse,
as chance and bravery merge in the art of war.
And yet Walthari's long spear held off the short sword
of his enemy. Gerwit wheeled his horse about
and tried to tire* his man so he could bring him down.

Now, as the anger grew and grew in Walthari,
he struck out, and knocked upwards Gerwit's shield,

Transmissoque femur penetraverat inguine ferrum.
Qui post terga ruens clamorem prodidit atrum
Exitiumque dolens pulsabat calcibus arvum.
Hunc etiam truncum caesa cervice reliquit.
940 Idem Wormatiae campis comes extitit ante.

Tum primum Franci coeperunt forte morari
Et magnis precibus dominum decedere pugna
Deposcunt. furit ille miser caecusque profatur:
'Quaeso, viri fortes et pectora saepe probata,
945 Ne fors haec cuicumque metum, sed conferat iram.
Quid mihi, si Vosago sic sic inglorius ibo?
Mentem quisque meam sibi vindicet. en ego partus
Ante mori sum, Wormatiam quam talibus actis
Ingrediar. petat hic patriam sine sanguine victor?
950 Hactenus arsistis hominem spoliare metallis,
Nunc ardete, viri, fusum mundare cruorem,
Ut mors abstergat mortem, sanguis quoque sanguem,
Soleturque necem sociorum plaga necantis.'

His animum dictis demens incendit et omnes
955 Fecerat immemores vitae simul atque salutis.
Ac velut in ludis alium praecurrere quisque
Ad mortem studuit, sed semita, ut antea dixi,
Cogebat binos bello decernere solos.

Vir tamen illustris dum cunctari videt illos,
960 Vertice distractas suspendit in arbore cristas
Et ventum captans sudorem tersit anhelus.

Ecce repentino Randolf athleta caballo
Praevertens reliquos hunc importunus adivit
Ac mox ferrato petiit sub pectore conto.
965 Et nisi duratis Wielandia fabrica giris
Obstaret, spisso penetraverit ilia ligno.

and then his blade thrust through the thigh, into the groin.
Gerwit fell backwards with a cry of agony,
bewailed his fate, drummed his heels on the ground, and died.*
Walthari left him lying as a headless trunk,
who once had been an Earl in the city of Worms.

For the first time the Franks began to hesitate,
and beg their lord, with fervent prayers, to stop
the fight. Bu wretched Gundahari in his blindness
raged: "You men are strong, your bravery is tried,
let these events cause anger and not instil fear!
How can I leave the Vosges inglorious in defeat?
May all of you adopt my attitude. I am
prepared to die rather than go back to my town
of Worms. Should he go home as victor quite unscathed?
Your burning wish till now was to gain this man's gold.
Now burn instead, my warriors, to avenge the blood.
Let there be death for death, let blood atone for blood,
and let the killer's death pay for the comrades killed!"

The king's crazed anger fuelled the fire in all their souls,
and made them careless of their lives, their will to live.
As if it were a race, each of them hurried on,
to get to—death. But as we know, the entrance-path
permitted only single combat, one to one.

When brave Walthari saw how they hesitated,
he took off his battle-helm and hung it in a tree,
and caught his breath again, and wiped away the sweat.

Then suddenly the warrior Randolf* leapt upon
his horse, and rushed ahead, before the other men,
and caught Walthari full-on with his iron-tipped spear.
Had Wayland's* work, Walthari's ring-mail, not withstood
the blow, the wooden spear-shaft would have done its worst.

Ille tamen subito stupefactus corda pavore
Munimen clipei obiecit mentemque recepit;
Nec tamen et galeam fuerat sumpsisse facultas.
970 Francus at emissa gladium nudaverat hasta
Et feriens binos Aquitani vertice crines
Abrasit, sed forte cutem praestringere summam
Non licuit, rursumque alium vibraverat ictum
Et praeceps animi directo obstamine scuti
975 Impegit calibem, nec quivit viribus ullis
Elicere. Alpharides retro, se fulminis instar
Excutiens, Francum valida vi fudit ad arvum
Et super assistens pectus conculcat et inquit:
'En pro calvitio capitis te vertice fraudo,
980 Ne fiat ista tuae de me iactantia sponsae.'
Vix effatus haec truncavit colla precantis.

At nonus pugnae Helmnod successit, et ipse
Insertum triplici gestabat fune tridentem,
Quem post terga quidem socii stantes tenuerunt,
985 Consiliumque fuit, dum cuspis missa sederet
In clipeo, cuncti pariter traxisse studerent,
Ut vel sic hominem deiecissent furibundum;
Atque sub hac certum sibi spe posuere triumphum.
Nec mora, dux totas fundens in brachia vires
990 Misit in adversum magna cum voce tridentem
Edicens: 'ferro tibi finis, calve, sub isto!'
Qui ventos penetrans iaculorum more coruscat,
Quod genus aspidis ex alta sese arbore tanto
Turbine demittit, quo cuncta obstantia vincat.
995 Quid moror? umbonem sciderat peltaque resedit.
Clamorem Franci tollunt saltusque resultat,
Obnixique trahunt restim simul atque vicissim,
Nec dubitat princeps tali se aptare labori.
Manarunt cunctis sudoris flumina membris.

Walthari, suddenly struck to the heart by fear,
brought up his shield, and took a grip upon himself,
but still he was unable to regain his helmet.
His spear now thrown, Randolf the Frank unsheathed his sword
struck out, and cut off two locks of Walthari's hair
although his sword did not reach to the warrior's skin;
and then he rapidly dealt him another blow
but all too rashly thrust his sword into the shield
raised in defense, and now, for all his strength, he could
not pull it out. Alphari's son, like lightning now
pulled back, then with great force hurled Randolf backwards
to the ground. He placed his foot upon the other's chest
and said: "For shaving my head you shall now lose yours,
or you would go and boast about me to your girl!"
No sooner said than done; he severed Randolf's neck.

The ninth man in the fight, Helmnot* came in, and he
fought with a trident, tied onto a threefold cord
held firmly by his comrades standing behind him.
His plan was that, once he had hit Walthari's shield
and it sat firm, the others then would pull together
and in that way would throw Walthari off his feet—
with this they hoped to gain a certain victory.
Without delay the leader threw with all his force,
and as the trident flew, he shouted at his enemy:
"This weapon, shaven-head, will be the end of you!"
The trident, cutting through the air, sparkled and shone
just like a serpent, those that strike from up a tree
at whirlwind speed and vanquish anything they meet.
Enough!* The trident hit and split the shield, but lodged.
The forests echoed with the sound of Frankish cries,
as they all pulled firmly and together on the cord—
the king himself joined without hesitation in the work.
Rivers of sweat poured down the limbs of every man.

111

1000 Sed tamen haec inter velut aesculus astitit heros,
Quae non plus petit astra comis quam Tartara fibris,
Contempnens omnes ventorum immota fragores.
Certabant hostes hortabanturque viritim,
Ut, si non quirent ipsum detrudere ad arvum,
1005 Munimen clipei saltem extorquere studerent,
Quo dempto vivus facile caperetur ab ipsis.
Nomina quae restant edicam iamque trahentum:
Nonus Eleuthir erat, Helmnod cognomine dictus,
Argentina quidem decimum dant oppida Trogum,
1010 Extulit undecimum pollens urbs Spira Tanastum,
Absque Haganone locum rex supplevit duodenum.
Quattuor hi adversum summis conatibus unum
Contendunt pariter multo varioque tumultu.

Interea Alpharidi vanus labor incutit iram,
1015 Et qui iam pridem nudarat casside frontem,
In framea tunicaque simul confisus aena
Omisit parmam primumque invasit Eleuthrin.
Huic galeam findens cerebrum diffudit et ipsam
Cervicem resecans pectus patefecit, at aegrum
1020 Cor pulsans animam liquit mox atque calorem.

Inde petit Trogum haerentem in fune nefando.
Qui subito attonitus recidentis morte sodalis
Horribilique hostis conspectu coeperat acrem
Nequiquam temptare fugam voluitque relicta
1025 Arma recolligere, ut rursum repararet agonem.
Nam cuncti funem tracturi deposuerunt
Hastas cum clipeis.) sed quanto maximus heros
Fortior extiterat, tanto fuit ocior, olli
Et cursu capto suras mucrone recidit
1030 Ac sic tardatum praevenit et abstulit eius
Scutum. sed Trogus, quamvis de vulnere lassus,
Mente tamen fervens saxum circumspicit ingens,

TRANSLATION

But all the time Walthari stood firm as an oak,
which seeks neither to reach the stars nor with its roots
touch Hell, but stands unmoved and scorns the stormy winds.
The enemy tugged, and urged each other on,
trying, if he could not be toppled to the ground,
at least to pull away his one defense, his shield,
for if he lost it, they could capture him alive.
What were the names of those men tugging at the cord?
The ninth attacker, Helmnot, known as Eleuthir,*
was there, and with him from the town of Strasbourg, Drogo,
tenth to fight. Tanasto, the eleventh, came from
bustling Speyer. The king was twelfth—instead of Hagano.
Four men fought here with all their force against one man,
struggling together and making a great noise.

Meanwhile, their fruitless efforts angered Walthari,
who had removed his helmet and had bared his head;
he put his trust in his ring-mail and his sword,
threw down his shield and attacked Helmnot* first of all.
He split his helmet so his brains spilled out, then hacked
his head off, and opened up his chest, so that
the heart, still pulsing, gave up all its life and warmth.

Drogo, who clung to the ill-fated cord, was next.
Already shocked by his comrade's sudden death,
and by the frightening appearance of his enemy,
he tried in vain to run, so he could gather up
the waiting weapons and come back into the fray—
for all of them, when they prepared to pull the rope,
had left their shields and spears—but just as Walthari
was stronger than the rest, he was much faster too.
He caught him up, and with his sword slashed Drogo's legs,
then, overtaking him, he knocked away his shield.
But Drogo, even though the wound had slowed him down,
burned with battle-fury. He spotted a great boulder,

Quod rapiens subito obnixum contorsit in hostem
Et proprium a summo clipeum fidit usque deorsum.
1035 Sed retinet fractum pellis superaddita lignum.
Moxque genu posito viridem vacuaverat aedem
Atque ardens animis vibratu terruit auras,
Et si non quivit virtutem ostendere factis,
Corde tamen habitum patefecit et ore virilem.
1040 Nec manes ridere videns audaciter infit:
'O mihi si clipeus vel sic modo adesset amicus!
Fors tibi victoriam de me, non inclita virtus
Contulit. ad scutum mucronem hic tollito nostrum!'

Tum quoque subridens 'venio iam' dixerat heros
1045 Et cursu advolitans dextram ferientis ademit.
Sed cum athleta ictum libraret ab aure secundum
Pergentique animae valvas aperire studeret,
Ecce Tanastus adest telis cum rege resumptis
Et socium obiecta protexit vulnere pelta.
1050 Hinc indignatus iram convertit in ipsum
Waltharius humerumque eius de cardine vellit
Perque latus ducto suffudit viscera ferro.
Ave! procumbens submurmurat ore Tanastus.
Quo recidente preces contempsit promere Trogus
1055 Conviciisque sui victorem incendit amaris,
Seu virtute animi, seu desperaverat. exin
Alpharides: 'morere' inquit 'et haec sub Tartara transfer
Enarrans sociis, quod tu sis ultus eosdem.'
His dictis torquem collo circumdedit aureum.
1060 Ecce simul caesi volvuntur pulvere amici,
Crebris foedatum ferientes calcibus arvum.

His rex infelix visis suspirat et omni
Aufugiens studio falerati terga caballi
Scandit et ad maestum citius Haganona volavit
1065 Omnimodisque illum precibus flexisse sategit,

picked it up, and hurled it at his adversary,
and split his shield from the top to the bottom.
But the covering of leather held the broken wood.
Drogo fell to his knees, but drew his sword out of
its copper-banded* sheath, and wildly slashed the air.
Now, though he could not show his bravery by deeds,
his words made clear the valor that was in his heart.
He did not see the smiling spirits of the dead,
but said: "If I had only reached my friendly shield!
Pure Fate has given you this victory, not force
of arms. You have my shield. Here, take my sword as well!"

Walthari, also smiling, answered: "Here I am!"
and running in, he hacked off the man's right hand.
But as Walthari swung his sword for a second blow,
so he could set free the man's departing spirit,
Tanasto and the king, who had retrieved their spears,
moved in to shield their fallen comrade from the blow.
Walthari, greatly angered, turned on Tanasto,
and tore his shoulder from its very socket,
then thrust his sword into his side and spilled his entrails.
As he sank down, Tanasto murmured just "Farewell!"
The fallen Drogo uttered not a single prayer,
but still hurled bitter taunts towards his conqueror,
either in desperation, or through bravery.
Walthari said: "And now you die. Go, take these words
to Hades, tell your friends how you avenged them!"
And then he put a blood-red line round Drogo's neck.*
See how the two dead friends lie twitching in the dust,
their heels* still knocking against the blood-soaked earth!

The ill-starred Gundahari* saw all this, and sighed,
then fled with all his speed to mount his horse,
that stood already saddled, and quickly rode to the brooding
Hagano to try and move him with his pleading

Ut secum pergens pugnam repararet. at ille:
'Me genus infandum prohibet bellare parentum,
Et gelidus sanguis mentem mihi ademit in armis.
Tabescebat enim genitor, dum tela videret,
1070 Et timidus multis renuebat proelia verbis:
Haec dum iactasses, rex, inter te comitantes,
Extitit indignum nostri tibi quippe iuvamen.'

Ille recusanti precibus nihilominus instans
Talibus aversum satagit revocare loquelis:
1075 'Deprecor ob superos, conceptum pone furorem.
Iram de nostra contractam decute culpa,
Quam vita comitante, domum si venero tecum,
Impensis tibimet benefactis diluo multis.
Nonne pudet sociis tot cognatisque peremptis
1080 Dissimulare virum? magis, ut mihi quippe videtur,
Verba valent animum quam facta nefanda movere.
Iustius in saevum tumuisses mente tyrannum,
Qui solus hodie caput infamaverat orbis.
Non modicum patimur dammum de caede virorum,
1085 Dedecus at tantum superabit Francia numquam.
Antea quis fuimus suspecti, sibila dantes
Francorum dicent exercitus omnis ab uno,
Proh pudor ignotum vel quo, est impune necatus!'

Cunctabatur adhuc Haganon et pectore sponsam
1090 Walthario plerumque fidem volvebat et ipsum
Eventum gestae recolebat in ordine causae.
Supplicius tamen infelix rex institit illi.
Cuius subnixe rogitantis acumine motus
Erubuit domini vultum, replicabat honorem
1095 Virtutis propriae, qui fors vilesceret inde,
Si quocumque modo in rebus sibi parceret istis.
Erupit tandem et clara sic voce respondit:

to come with him and to renew the light. Hagano*
said: "My much-scorned ancestry will not let me fight,
my blood runs cold at the thought of joining battle;
my father fainted if he so much as saw a sword,
so timid, he would talk his way out of all fights.
When you said things like that before our comrades, king,
you did not seem to place great value on my help!"

The king went on imploring his reluctant friend,
and tried to change his mind by using words like these:
"By the Gods above, please put aside your rage,
give up this anger, the fault for which was mine,
and if I live, and we should reach our home together
I shall make good the wrong with many great rewards.
And are you not ashamed, when friends and kin are dead,
to lie about your bravery? But still it seems to me
that words, not evil deeds will stir your soul to act.
It would be juster if your bitterness were aimed
at him who has today brought me, your king,* to shame.
The death of all our men is no small injury,
but can the Franks ever get over such disgrace?
People who feared us once will now be whispering
of how a single unknown man could be allowed to kill
a Frankish army, and all—for shame!—without revenge!"

Hagano hesitated. In his heart and mind
he turned over the loyalty pledged to Walthari
and thought about the day's events in order. Still
the unhappy king continued to plead with him.
They dismounted, and then let the horses graze.
Moved by the sharpness of the king's entreating,
he blushed* before his lord, and thought about his honor
as a warrior, which might be tarnished if
in any way he were to try to spare himself.
And then at last he cried out in a ringing voice:

'Quo me, domne, vocas? quo te sequar, inclite princeps?
Quae nequeunt fieri, spondet fiducia cordi.
1100 Quis tam desipiens quandoque fuisse probatur,
Qui saltu baratrum sponte attemptarit apertum?
Nam scio Waltharium per campos sic fore acerbum,
Ut tali castro nec non statione locatus
Ingentem cuneum velut unum temnat homullum.
1105 Et licet huc cunctos equites simul atque pedestres
Francia misisset, sic his ceu fecerat istis.
Sed quia conspicio te plus doluisse pudore
Quam caedis damno nec sic discedere velle,
Compatior propriusque dolor succumbit honori
1110 Regis: et ecce viam conor reperire salutis,
Quae tamen aut nusquam ostendit se sive coacte.
Nam propter carum (fateor tibi, domne) nepotem
Promissam fidei normam corrumpere nollem.
Ecce in non dubium pro te, rex, ibo periclum.
1115 Ast hic me penitus conflictu cedere noris.
Secedamus eique locum praestemus eundi
Et positi in speculis tondamus prata caballis,
Donec iam castrum securus deserat artum,
Nos abiisse ratus. campos ubi calcet apertos,
1120 Insurgamus et attonitum post terga sequamur:
Sic aliquod virtutis opus temptare valemus.
Haec mihi in ambiguis spes est certissima rebus.
Tum pugnare potes, belli si, rex, tibi mens est:
Quippe fugam nobis numquam dabit ille duobus,
1125 At nos aut fugere aut acrum bellare necesse est.'
Laudat consilium satrapa et complectitur illum
Osculoque virum demulcet; et ecce recedunt
Insidiisque locum circumspexere sat aptum
Demissique ligant animalia gramine laeto.

1130 Interea occiduas vergebat Phoebus in oras,
Ultima per notam signans vestigia Thilen,

TRANSLATION

"Where do you call me, lord? Where shall I follow my
great prince? Confidence makes what cannot be done seem
possible. What man would show himself as such a fool
as to leap, of his own accord, into the abyss?
I know Walthari; in the open field he is
so fierce, that, in a stronghold such as he holds now,
he would disdain a troop just like a single dwarf.
And even if the Franks sent all their soldiers in,
both foot and cavalry, their treatment would be the same.
But since I see that you are more distressed by shame
than loss of men, and therefore will not go away,
my feelings are with you, and my own sadness bows
before the honor of a king. So I shall try
to find a way to save us, which must be now or never.
I say this to you, lord: not for my dear nephew
would I be willing to break faith with Walthari.
For you, O king, I undertake the certain dangers!
But know that I refuse to fight him in this place.
Let us withdraw, give him the chance to move away,
then keep a lookout as we let the horses graze,
till he feels safe enough to come out of his camp,
thinking us gone. And when he sets foot in open field
we take him by surprise, ambush him from behind*—
that way we can bring off a noble deed of arms.
For me this is the best plan in our present case.
Then you can fight Walthari if you will, O king.
He will not want to try and flee, just from two men,
so we shall either have to run or stay and fight."
King Gundahari praised the strategy, then embraced
and soothed his vassal with a kiss. Next, they withdrew
to find a place that would be suitable for ambush.
They dismounted, and then let the horses graze.

Meanwhile, the sun was now inclining in the west,
touching distant and famous Thule with its last rays,

Et cum Scottigenis post terga reliquit Hiberos.
Hic postquam oceanas sensim calefecerat undas,
Hesperos Ausonidis obvertit cornua terris,
1135 Tum secum sapiens coepit tractare satelles,
Utrum sub tuto per densa silentia castro
Sisteret, an vastis heremi committeret arvis.
Aestuat immensis curarum fluctibus, et quid
Iam faceret, sollers arguta indagine quaerit.
1140 Solus enim Hagano fuerat suspectus et illud
Oscillum regis subter complexibus actum.
Ambierat prorsus, quae sit sententia menti
Hostis et an urbem vellent remeare relictam,
Pluribus ut sociis per noctem forte coactis
1145 Primo mane parent bellum recreare nefandum
An soli insidias facerent propiusque laterent.
Terret ad haec triviis ignoti silva meatus,
Ne loca fortassis incurreret aspera spinis,
Immo quippe feris, sponsamque amitteret illis.

1150 His ita provisis exploratisque profatur:
'En quocumque modo res pergant, hic recubabo,
Donec circuiens lumen spera reddat amatum,
Ne patriae fines dicat rex ille superbus
Evasisse fuga furis de more per umbras.'
1155 Dixit et ecce viam vallo praemuniit artam
Undique praecisis spinis simul et paliuris.
Quo facto ad truncos sese convertit amaro
Cum gemitu et cuicumque suum caput applicat atque
Contra orientalem prostratus corpore partem
1160 Ac nudum retinens ensem hac voce precatur:
'Rerum factori, sed et omnia facta regenti,
Nil sine permisso cuius vel denique iusso
Constat, ago grates, quod me defendit iniquis
Hostilis turmae telis nec non quoque probris.
1165 Deprecor at dominum contrita mente benignum,

and passing from Ireland and from the edge of Spain.*
Now when it had lit up and warmed the ocean's waves,
the Evening Star* pointed its rays towards Italy,
while Walthari wisely began to consider
if he should stay there in the silence of his camp
or venture out into the great and open wilderness.
Waves of uncertainty swept across his mind; he
wondered what to do, and weighed it up carefully.
Suspicions were aroused by Hagano alone,
and by that kiss, given in the king's embrace.
He had no real idea of what was in the minds
of his enemies; did they plan to return to Worms,
and overnight to gather up more warriors
so that at dawn they could renew the wicked fight?
Or were they still nearby, to ambush him alone?
The woodland worried him as well, with its winding tracks,
where he might run against impenetrable thorns,
or where wild beasts might carry off his beloved.

He thought about all this and weighed it in his mind,
and said: "However things turn out, I shall lie down
in this place until the sun's light comes round again,
so that the tyrant king can never say I fled
his homeland in the shadowed darkness, like a thief."
With that, he built a barrier-wall for the defile,
made out of spiky thorns, and hawthorn* bushes, too.
Then he turned to the headless bodies with a sigh
of bitterness, and placed each head back with its corpse.
He threw himself upon the ground, and facing east
he prayed aloud, holding his bare sword in his hand:
"To God, who made all things, and who controls all deeds,
and without whose command no things exist at all,
I now give thanks for shielding me from the weapons
of all my enemies, and from their shameful deeds.
O kindly God, I pray with contrite heart that He

Ut qui peccantes non vult sed perdere culpas,
Hos in caelesti praestet mihi sede videri.'
Qui postquam orandi finem dedit, ilico surgens
Sex giravit equos et virgis rite retortis
1170 Vinciit: hi tantum remanebant, nempe duobus
Per tela absumptis ternos rex Gunthere abegit.

His ita compositis procinctum solvit et alte
Ingenti fumans leviabat pondere corpus.
Tum maestam laeto solans affamine sponsam
1175 Moxque cibum capiens aegros recreaverat artus,
Oppido enim lassus fuerat, clipeoque recumbens
Primi custodem somni iubet esse puellam,
Ipse matutinam disponens tollere curam,
Quae fuerat suspecta magis, tandemque quievit.
1180 Ad cuius caput illa sedens solito vigilavit
Et dormitantes cantu patefecit ocellos.
Ast ubi vir primum iam expergiscendo soporem
Ruperat, absque mora surgens dormire puellam
Iussit et arrepta se fulciit impiger hasta.
1185 Sic reliquum noctis duxit, modo quippe caballos
Circuit, interdum auscultans vallo propiavit,
Exoptans orbi species ac lumina reddi.

Lucifer interea praeco scandebat Olympo
Dicens: 'Taprobane clarum videt insula solem.'
1190 Hora fuit, gelidus qua terram irrorat Eous.
Aggreditur iuvenis caesos spoliarier armis
Armorumque habitu, tunicas et cetera linquens:
Armillas tantum, cum bullis baltea et enses,
Loricas quoque cum galeis detraxerat ollis.
1195 Quattuor His oneravit equos sponsamque vocatam
Imposuit quinto, sextum conscenderat ipse
Et primus vallo perrexerat ipse revulso.
At dum constricti penetratur semita callis,

who wishes to destroy the sins but not the sinner
may let me see them all once more in Heaven's realms.
When he had finished all his prayers, Walthari rose
and rounded up six horses, tethering them then
with plaited reed. Only these six remained, for two
had been killed, and the king* had driven three away.

Now that he had decided, he undid his sword-belt,
and took the heavy armor from his sweating body.
Calming his frightened love with encouraging words,
he quickly ate, refreshed his battle-weary limbs
—he was exhausted—and then, resting on his shield,
he told the girl to stand guard first, while he was sleeping.
He himself, however, would take the morning watch,
which was more dangerous; and then at last he slept.
So Hildigunda held vigil, sitting at his head,
and kept herself awake by singing to herself.
Walthari woke, and cut short the first spell of sleep,
got up without delay, and told the girl to rest,
while he stood guard, resting upon his snatched-up spear.
And thus he spent the night. From time to time, he checked
the horses and listened at his barricade,
longing for sight and the sunlight to be restored.

And then the herald Daystar* rose above Olympus,
announcing sunrise over India and the east;
it was the hour when cool dawn puts dew on the earth.
The young warrior set to, stripping the dead of arms
and weapons, leaving behind their tunics and the rest.
He took their arm-rings, buckled belts and swords,
mail-coats and helmets too (but no more than these)
and loaded four horses. He called Hildigunda
and put her on the fifth, whilst he mounted the sixth*
and rode out first, having torn down his barricade.
But always as he rode along the narrow path,

Circumquaque oculis explorans omnia puris
1200 Auribus arrectis ventos captavit et auras,
Si vel mussantes sentiret vel gradientes
Sive superborum crepitantia frena virorum,
Seu saltim ferrata sonum daret ungula equorum.

Postquam cuncta silere videt, praevortit onustas
1205 Quadrupedes, mulierem etiam praecedere iussit.
Scrinia gestantem comprendens ipse caballum
Audet inire viam consueto cinctus amictu.
Mille fere passus transcendit, et ecce puella
Sexus enim fragilis animo trepidare coegit—
1210 Respiciens post terga videt descendere binos
Quodam colle viros raptim et sine more meantes
Exanguisque virum compellat voce sequentem:
'Dilatus iam finis adest: fuge, domne, propinquant!'
Qui mox conversus visos cognovit et inquit:
1215 'Incassum multos mea dextera fuderat hostes,
Si modo supremis laus desit, dedecus assit,
Est satius pulcram per vulnera quaerere mortem
Quam solum amissis palando evadere rebus.
Verum non adeo sunt desperanda salutis
1220 Commoda cernenti quondam maiora pericla.
Aurum gestantis tute accipe lora Leonis
Et citius pergens luco succede propinquo.
Ast ego in ascensu montis subsistere malo,
Eventum opperiens adventantesque salutans.'
1225 Obsequitur dictis virguncula clara iubentis.
Ille celer scutum collegit et excutit hastam,
Ignoti mores equitis temptando sub armis.

Hunc rex incursans comitante satellite demens
Eminus affatu compellat valde superbo:
1230 'Hostis atrox, nisu deluderis! ecce latebrae
Protinus absistunt, ex quis de more liciscae

looking about him carefully to every side,
he listened sharply to every breeze and breath of wind,
in case he heard men whispering or coming near,
or caught the jingling sound of proud warriors' bridles,
or at least the noise of a horse's iron-shod hoof.

He saw that all was quiet, then he sent the laden
horses out, and told the woman she should ride ahead.
He led the horse himself which carried the two chests,
and risked setting out, dressed in his usual armor.
They had gone about a thousand paces when the girl
(whose sex, the weaker, made her a greater prey to fear)
looked backward, and then saw two men come riding down
one of the hills, and riding fast and hard; she paled
with fright, and called out to the man who followed her:
"Although we held it off, our end has come! Lord, flee,
they are coming closer!" He turned and knew their faces.
"My right hand would have killed so many enemies
in vain," he said, "if these last brought me shame, not glory.
Better to seek a decent death, cut down by wounds,
than to lose everything, just to escape alone.
Nor is the situation quite so desperate
for someone who has faced far greater dangers.
You must lead Lion, and take him with the gold
as quickly as you can, to hide in the next grove.
But I would rather stand here on the mountain-side
to see what happens, and to meet and greet these men."
The young and beautiful princess did as he said.
Quickly he took his shield, and hefted his battle-spear
to see how his untried horse behaved under arms.

The crazed king, rushing for him with his vassal,
shouted in arrogance while he was still far off:
"Most wicked enemy, you have fought your last!
Your hiding-place is far away, the one from which

Dentibus infrendens rabidis latrare solebas.
En in propatulo, si vis, confligito campo,
Experiens, finis si fors queat aequiperari
1235 Principio. scio, Fortunam mercede vocasti
Idcircoque fugam tempnis seu deditionem.'

Alpharides contra regi non reddidit ulla,
Sed velut hinc surdus alio convertitur aiens:
'Ad te sermo mihi, Hagano, subsiste parumper!
1240 Quid, rogo, tam fidum subito mutavit amicum,
Ut, discessurus nuper vix posse revelli
Qui nostris visus fuerat complexibus, ultro,
Nullis nempe malis laesus, nos appetat armis?
Sperabam, fateor, de te,—sed denique fallor—,
1245 Quod si de exilio redeuntem nosse valeres,
Ipse salutatum mihimet mox obvius ires
Et licet invitum hospitii requiete foveres
Pacificeque in regna patris deducere velles;
Sollicitusque fui, quorsum tua munera ferrem.
1250 Namque per ignotas dixi pergens regiones:
Francorum vereor Haganone superstite nullum.
Obsecro per ludos, resipiscito iam, pueriles,
Unanimes quibus assueti fuimusque periti
Et quorum cultu primos attrivimus annos.
1255 Inclita quonam migravit concordia nobis
Semper in hoste domique manens nec scandala noscens?
Quippe tui facies patris obliviscier egit,
Tecum degenti mihi patria viluit ampla.
Numquid mente fidem abradis saepissime pactam?
1260 Deprecor, hoc abscide nefas neu bella lacessas
Sitque inconvulsum nobis per tempora foedus.
Quod si consentis, iam nunc ditatus abibis
Eulogiis, rutilo umbonem complebo metallo.'

Contra quae Hagano vultu haec affamina torvo

TRANSLATION

you bared your teeth and barked just like a rabid* dog.
So fight now, if you dare,* out in the open field.
See if your battles end the way that they began!
I know you think the Goddess Fortune is your whore,*
and it would not occur to you to run or to surrender!"

The son of Alphari did not answer the king,
but, like a deaf man, turned, and to the other said:
"My words are for your ears, Hagano. Stand! Wait!
I wonder why a faithful friend changes so suddenly
that he, who, when we parted not so long ago,
could barely (so it seemed) leave me of his free will,
can now attack me, though I have done him no harm?
I used to hope of you—but then, I was deceived—
that if I came from exile, and you heard of this,
you would ride out to be the first to welcome me,
and offer hospitality and rest, even
if I demurred, and escort me to my father's lands.
I even worried how I could bring you my gifts!
As I rode through the unknown lands, I told myself:
I fear no Franks if Hagano is still alive!
Now think, I beg you, how when we were boys we played
together, the games we had in happy harmony,
and how we trained together in those early years!
Where is that famous comradeship we used to have
which knew no breach, at home or on the battlefield?
Being with you, I even managed to forget
my father, and my native country counted less.
Have you cut from your heart the faith we swore so often?
Please, put this wickedness aside and do not fight,
and let our friendship stand unbroken for all time.
If you will but agree, then you will go away
laden with gifts, and with your shield filled with red gold."

Hagano, grim-faced, made reply to this, and with

1265 Edidit atque iram sic insinuavit apertam:
'Vim prius exerces, Walthari, postque sopharis.
Tute fidem abscideras, cum memet adesse videres
Et tot stravisses socios immoque propinquos.
Excusare nequis, quin me tunc affore nosses.
1270 Cuius si facies latuit, tamen arma videbas
Nota satis habituque virum rescire valebas.
Cetera fors tulerim, si vel dolor unus abesset:
Unice enim carum rutilum blandum pretiosum
Carpsisti florem mucronis falce tenellum.
1275 Haec res est, pactum qua irritasti prior almum,
Circoque gazam cupio pro foedere nullam.
Sitne tibi soli virtus, volo discere in armis,
Deque tuis manibus caedem perquiro nepotis.
En aut oppeto sive aliquid memorabile faxo.'

1280 Dixit et a tergo saltu se iecit equino,
Hoc et Guntharius nec segnior egerat heros
Waltharius, cuncti pedites bellare parati.
Stabat quisque ac venturo se providus ictu
Praestruxit: trepidant sub peltis Martia membra.

1285 Hora secunda fuit, qua tres hi congrediuntur,
Adversus solum conspirant arma duorum.
Primus maligeram collectis viribus hastam
Direxit Hagano disrupta pace. sed illam
Turbine terribilem tanto et stridore volantem
1290 Alpharides semet cernens tolerare nequire
Sollers obliqui delusit tegmine scuti:
Nam veniens clipeo sic est ceu marmore levi
Excussa et collem vehementer sauciat usque
Ad clavos infixa solo. tunc pectore magno,
1295 Sed modica vi fraxineum hastile superbus
Iecit Guntharius, volitans quod adhaesit in ima
Waltharii parma, quam mox dum concutit ipse,
Excidit ignavum de ligni vulnere ferrum.

his words made plain the anger that he felt. He said:
"First violence, Walthari, and now sophistry!
It was you broke the trust when you saw I was here,
and killed so many of those near and dear to me.
Nor can you claim my presence was unknown to you,
for you could see my weapons, even if my face
was hidden. But I could have borne all things, but one:
the sorrow that my one dear, precious blooming flower*
was mown down by the sickle of your sword;
and by that deed you were the first to break our trust.
I want no treasure as a mark of friendship now.
I shall find out in fighting if your courage holds,
and take from your hands payment for my nephew's blood.
Either I fall, or I shall do great deeds of arms."

With these words he leapt quickly from his horse's back
and Gundahari did so too; nor did Walthari
wait, and now all three on foot prepared to fight.
Each stood his ground and waited for the blow to fall
and each of them trembled beneath his shield.

It was the second hour* of daylight when they fought,
two men in arms standing against a single man.
With all his strength Hagano hurled his wicked* spear
and thus was first to break the peace. But Walthari,*
who knew that he could not withstand it as it flew
with terrifying whirlwind force and roaring noise,
slanted his shield, and managed to deflect its course.
The spear came, but glanced off his shield as if
from polished marble, cut a wound into the hill
and stuck* there fast. Next, very boldly, but with far less
force, the arrogant king Gundahari hurled his
ash-wood spear, which in its flight struck at the base
of the other's shield; but when Walthari shook it
the iron lance fell harmless from the wounded wood.

Omine quo maesti confuso pectore Franci
1300 Mox stringunt acies, dolor est conversus ad iras,
Et tecti clipeis Aquitanum invadere certant.
Strennuus ille tamen vi cuspidis expulit illos
Atque incursantes vultu terrebat et armis.
Hic rex Guntharius coeptum meditatur ineptum,
1305 Scilicet ut iactam frustra terraeque relapsam,
Ante pedes herois enim divulsa iacebat—,
Accedens tacite furtim sustolleret hastam,
Quandoquidem brevibus gladiorum denique telis
Armati nequeunt accedere comminus illi,
1310 Qui tam porrectum torquebat cuspidis ictum.
Innuit ergo oculis vassum praecedere suadens,
Cuius defensu causam supplere valeret.

Nec mora, progreditur Haganon ac provocat hostem,
Rex quoque gemmatum vaginae condidit ensem,
1315 Expediens dextram furto actutum faciendo.
Sed quid plura? manum pronus transmisit in hastam
Et iam comprensam sensim subtraxerat illam
Fortunae maiora petens. sed maximus heros,
Utpote qui bello semper sat providus esset
1320 Praeter et unius punctum cautissimus horae,
Hunc inclinari cernens persenserat actum
Nec tulit, obstantem sed mox Haganona revellens,
Denique sublato qui divertebat ab ictu,
Insilit et planta direptum hastile retentat
1325 Ac regem furto captum sic increpitavit,
Ut iam perculso sub cuspide genva labarent.
Quem quoque continuo esurienti porgeret Orco,
Ni Hagano armipotens citius succurreret atque
Obiecto dominum scuto muniret et hosti
1330 Nudam aciem saevi mucronis in ora tulisset.
Sic, dum Waltharius vulnus cavet, ille resurgit
Atque tremens studiusque stetit, vix morte reversus.

TRANSLATION

The Franks were both disheartened by this omen
but quickly drew their swords as sorrow turned to rage.
Behind their shields they now attacked the Aquitanian.
He drove them back with the force of his great spear,
his weapons terrifying, and his aspect grim.
King Gundahari now conceived a foolish plan.
In order to retrieve the spear he threw in vain,
which now lay, shaken from the hero's shield, by his feet
he tried approaching silently and stealthily;
for someone who is armed with only a short sword
cannot move openly to come close to a man
wielding a spear, a weapon with a greater reach.
He caught his vassal's eye, and motioned him to move
ahead, hoping with his cover to carry out the deed.

Hagano moved at once, and challenged the enemy.
Meanwhile the king put in its sheath his jewelled sword,
to free his right hand, so that he could bring it off.
But now? He crouched, and stretched his hand out to the spear
and grasped it, pulling it towards him carefully,
hoping his luck would hold. But the hero Walthari,
who always fought with circumspection and the greatest
caution (dropping his guard just once,* as we shall hear),
saw the king stoop, realised what he intended,
and prevented it; he quickly drove off Hagano,
who tried to block him, but retreated from the blows,
sprang out and placed his foot onto the fallen spear.
He roared out at the king, caught in the very act,
whose knees were weak with terror as he faced the spear.
Walthari would have sent him straight to hungry Hell
had Hagano not run to give him aid in arms,
and to protect his lord by shielding him, swinging
his naked sword-blade in the face of the enemy.
Thus, while Walthari dodged the blow, the king got up
and stood trembling and speechless at his brush with death.

Nec mora nec requies: bellum instauratur amarum,
Incurrunt hominem nunc ambo nuncque vicissim;
1335 Et dum progresso se impenderet acrius uni,
En de parte alia subit alter et impedit ictum.
Haud aliter, Numidus quam dum venabitur ursus
Et canibus circumdatus astat et artubus horret
Et caput occultans submurmurat ac propiantes
1340 Amplexans Umbros miserum mutire coartat,
Tum rabidi circumlatrant hinc inde Molossi
Comminus ac dirae metuunt accedere belvae—,
Taliter in nonam conflictus fluxerat horam,
Et triplex cunctis inerat maceratio: leti
1345 Terror, et ipse labor bellandi, solis et ardor.

Interea herois coepit subrepere menti
Quiddam, qui tacito premit has sub corde loquelas:
'Si Fortuna viam non commutaverit, isti
Vana fatigatum memet per ludicra fallent.'
1360 Ilico et elata Haganoni voce profatur:
'O paliure, vires foliis, ut pungere possis;
Tu saltando iocans astu me ludere temptas.
Sed iam faxo locum, propius ne accedere tardes:
Ecce tuas—scio, praegrandes—ostendito vires!
1355 Me piget incassum tantos sufferre labores.'
Dixit et exiliens contum contorsit in ipsum,
Qui pergens onerat clipeum dirimitque aliquantum
Loricae ac magno modicum de corpore stringit;
Denique praecipuis praecinctus fulserat armis.

1360 At vir Waltharius missa cum cuspide currens
Evaginato regem importunior ense
Petit et scuto dextra de parte revulso
Ictum praevalidum ac mirandum fecit eique
Crus cum poplite adusque femur decerpserat omne.
1365 Ille super parmam ante pedes mox concidit huius.

No pauses and no rest. The bitter fight went on.
The two attacked their foe together or by turns,
and as he boldly struck out when one man advanced,
the other moved in from elsewhere to deflect the blow.
The scene was like the hunt of a Numidian bear,*
which, when held at bay by dogs, threatens with its claws,
lowers its head and growls, and takes a firm hold
of any Umbrian dog in reach, and makes it howl.
The wild Molossian hounds surround the bear, barking,
but afraid to come in too close to the wild beast.
So, some hours after noon,* the battle-tide was flowing
back and forth. A threefold misery gripped them all:
rank fear, the labor of fighting, and the sun's blaze.

And now a thought came into Walthari's mind,
and in his heart of hearts, he said to himself:
"If my fortune does not change its course, then these men
will trap me, tired as I am, by some ruse."
He turned to Hagano, and shouted with raised voice:
"Hawthorn,* your leaves and spines grow green, and you can sting!
You joke and jump about to get the best of me,
but I shall grant you space: come closer, don't delay,
come on, show me your strength—I know it is not small!
This effort, all of it in vain, is vexing me."
When he had spoken, he ran out and hurled his spear
at him; it flew and struck* his shield, and broke a piece
of armor, but stripped only a small part from his flesh,
for Hagano was well-armed all around his body.

Walthari, now his spear had been thrown, went running
and with drawn sword launched an attack on the king,
knocked his shield from the right, and with an amazing
sword-stroke, brought off with immense strength, he hacked off his
whole leg, with the knee, up to his thigh. The king fell
forward on his shield, right at Walthari's feet.

Palluit exanguis domino recidente satelles.
Alpharides spatam tollens iterato cruentam
Ardebat lapso postremum infligere vulnus.
Immemor at proprii Hagano vir forte doloris
1370 Aeratum caput inclinans obiecit ad ictum.
Extensam cohibere manum non quiverat heros,
Sed cassis fabrefacta diu meliusque peracta
Excipit assultum mox et scintillat in altum.
Cuius duritia stupefactus dissilit ensis,
1375 Proh dolor! et crepitans partim micat aere et herbis.

Belliger ut frameae murcatae fragmina vidit,
Indigne tulit ac nimia furit efferus ira
Impatiensque sui capulum sine pondere ferri,
Quamlibet eximio praestaret et arte metallo,
1380 Protinus abiecit monimentaque tristia sprevit.
Qui dum forte manum iam enormiter exeruisset,
Abstulit hanc Hagano sat laetus vulnere prompto.
In medio iactus recidebat dextera fortis
Gentibus ac populis multis suspecta, tyrannis,
1385 Innumerabilibus quae fulserat ante trophaeis.
Sed vir praecipuus nec laevis cedere gnarus,
Sana mente potens carnis superare dolores,
Non desperavit neque vultus concidit eius,
Verum vulnigeram clipeo insertaverat ulnam
1390 Incolomique manu mox eripuit semispatam,
Qua dextrum cinxisse latus memoravimus illum,
Ilico vindictam capiens ex hoste severam.
Nam feriens dextrum Haganoni effodit ocellum
Ac timpus resecans pariterque labella revellens
1395 Olli bis ternos discussit ab ore molares.

Tali negotio dirimuntur proelia facto.
Quemque suum vulnus atque aeger anhelitus arma
Ponere persuasit. quisnam hinc immunis abiret,

TRANSLATION

When his lord fell, his vassal's blood drained from his face.
Alphari's son swung back his sword a second time,
wishing to give the final wound to the fallen man.
But Hagano, heedless of his own suffering,
leaned in, and let his own bronze helmet block the blow.
Walthari could not hold back his own outstretched arm,
and struck the finely-made and ancient helmet
such a blow that straight away the sparks flew up,
but its astounding hardness shattered the sword-blade—
alas!—pieces gleamed in the air and on the grass.

The warrior saw the fragments of his shattered sword*
with fury, and a great anger overcame him;
impatiently, holding a hilt which had now lost
its weight of iron, though it was well made and of gold,
he hurled it from him, scorning the wretched pieces.
But as he did so he by chance stretched out his hand;
Hagano, seeing a happy chance, hacked it off.
In mid-throw, Walthari's strong right hand was lost,
a hand that tribes, nations, and kings had feared,
and which had won innumerable victories.
But the great warrior never gave way to ill-luck;
his mind able to rise above his body's pain,
he did not despair, nor did his face as much as change.
He pushed his wounded arm into the grip of his shield,
and with his unscathed hand he drew out the short sword
which—you recall—he had strapped on at his right side,
and with it took stern vengeance on his enemy.
He struck out with a blow Hagano's right eye,
then slashed into his temple and tore apart his lip,
knocking twice three* back-teeth out of Hagano's mouth.

With this exchange, the battle now came to an end.
Wounds and exhausted weariness prompted each man
to lay down his arms. No one could have left unharmed

Qua duo magnanimi heroes tam viribus aequi
1400 Quam fervore animi steterant in fulmine belli?

Postquam finis adest, insignia quemque notabant:
Illic Guntharii regis pes, palma iacebat
Waltharii nec non tremulus Haganonis ocellus.
Sic sic armillas partiti sunt Avarenses!

1405 Consedere duo, nam tertius ille iacebat,
Sanguinis undantem tergentes floribus amnem.
Haec inter timidam revocat clamore puellam
Alpharides, veniens quae saucia quaeque ligavit.

His ita compositis sponsus praecepit eidem:
1410 'Iam misceto merum Haganoni et porrige primum;
Est athleta bonus, fidei si iura reservet.
Tum praebeto mihi, reliquis qui plus toleravi.
Postremum volo Guntharius bibat, utpote segnis
Inter magnanimum qui paruit arma virorum
1415 Et qui Martis opus tepide atque enerviter egit.'
Obsequitur cunctis Heririci filia verbis.
Francus at oblato licet arens pectore vino
Defer' ait 'prius Alpharidi sponso ac seniori,
Virgo, tuo, quoniam, fateor, me fortior ille
1420 Nec solum me, sed cunctos supereminet armis.'

Hic tandem Hagano spinosus et ipse Aquitanus,
Mentibus invicti, licet omni corpore lassi,
Post varios pugnae strepitus ictusque tremendos
Inter pocula scurrili certamine ludunt.
1425 Francus ait: 'iam dehinc cervos agitabis, amice,
Quorum de corio wantis sine fine fruaris:
At dextrum, moneo, tenera lanugine comple,
Ut causae ignaros palmae sub imagine fallas.
Wah! sed quid dicis, quod ritum infringere gentis

when two fierce heroes, just as equal in their strength
as fervor, stood and fought in the thunder of war.

The end had come. Each of the warriors was marked.
The leg of Gundahari lay there, the severed hand
of Walthari, and Hagano's still-quivering eye.
Thus — thus the golden arm-rings of the Huns were shared!

Two of the men sat down (the third was forced to lie)
and tried to staunch with foliage the flow of blood.
Then Walthari called with a shout the frightened girl,
and when she came to them, she bound up all their wounds.

When this had all been done, Walthari said to her:
"Now pour out wine, and serve Hagano first of all,
—he is a fine warrior if he keeps the laws of faith—
then pour for me, I have endured more than the others.
I think that Gundahari should drink last, who fought
with smaller effort in the trial of manly arms,
and did the work of Mars in a weak and lukewarm way."
The daughter of Heririk did as she was asked,
but when she gave wine to the Frank, although his throat burned,
he said: "Girl, give it first to your lord and betrothed,
Alphari's son; I say he is the stronger man—
he towers in arms over all men, not me alone.

Then Hagano the Thorny* and the Aquitanian,
their spirits high, although their bodies were weary
after the many blows and clashes of the fight,
played as they drank, and made fun of each other.
The Frank said: "From now on, when you hunt stag, my friend,
you can make gloves, as many as you like, from their skin.
But I suggest you stuff the right glove with soft wool,
and with this false hand deceive those who do not know!
Mind you*—what do you say about the breach of custom,

1430 Ac dextro femori gladium agglomerare videris
Uxorique tuae, si quando ea cura subintrat,
Perverso amplexu circumdabis euge sinistram?
Iam quid demoror? en posthac tibi quicquid agendum est,
Laeva manus faciet.' cui Walthare talia reddit:
1435 Cur tam prosilias, admiror, lusce Sicamber:
Si venor cervos, carnem vitabis aprinam.
Ex hoc iam famulis tu suspectando iubebis
Heroum turbas transversa tuendo salutans.
Sed fidei memor antiquae tibi consiliabor:
1440 Iam si quando domum venias laribusque propinques,
Effice lardatam de multra farreque pultam:
Haec pariter victum tibi conferet atque medelam.

His dictis pactum renovant iterato coactum
Atque simul regem tollentes valde dolentem
1445 Imponunt equiti et sic disiecti redierunt
Franci Wormatiam patriamque Aquitanus adivit.
Illic gratifice magno susceptus honore
Publica Hiltgundi fecit sponsalia rite
Omnibus et carus post mortem obitumque parentis
1450 Rexit ter denis populum feliciter annis.
Qualia bella dehinc vel quantos saepe triumphos
Ceperit, ecce stilus renuit signare retunsus.

Haec quicunque legis, stridenti ignosce cicadae
Raucellam nec adhuc vocem perpende, sed aevum,
1455 Utpote quae nidis nondum petit alta relictis.
Haec est Waltharii poesis. vos salvet Iesus.

TERMINAT LIBER DUORUM SODALIUM
WALTHARII ET HAGANONIS

when your people see your sword strapped to your right thigh?
And what about your wife, when desire comes over you
and you, alas! must put your awkward left arm round her?
But I am rambling! Everything that must be done
will now be done left-handed." Walthari* countered:
"I wonder that you make these jibes, you one-eyed Frank!*
I may hunt stag, but you can eat boar's flesh no more.
Signals to your servants will now be a sideways look,
and you will have to greet your warriors one-sidedly.
But, mindful of our old alliance, here is some
advice: when you get to your hearth and home again,
make porridge out of flour, milk, oats and bacon-fat,
and use it for your dinner and a poultice too!"

This said, they made their pact of friendship new again,
and as they did so, took the gravely wounded king
and put him on a horse; and thus they parted for
their homes, the Franks to Worms, the other to his land
of Aquitaine. There he was welcomed with great honor,
and was betrothed in public to Hildigunda.
Then, loved as he was by all, after his father's death
he ruled his people happily for thirty years.*
How many wars he won, how many victories were
gained afterwards, my pen is too blunt to record!

Dear reader! Please forgive the chirpings of a cricket,
ignore its grating little voice; take age into account!
It tried great things, though it had barely* left the nest.
That was Walthari's tale.* May Jesus save your souls.

HERE ENDS THE BOOK OF THE TWO ALLIES,
WALTHARI AND HAGANO*

NOTES

References in the notes are to the works listed in the bibliography; those to Gillespie are to his *Catalogue of Persons* (1973). In addition to Gillespie's catalogue, readers can find entries for some of this work's personages in the encyclopaedia of *The Nibelungen Tradition* (Gentry et al. 2002).

GERALD'S PROLOGUE

8 *irk*: Bate (1978) points out that the line contains a pun on Erkambald's name (*erchan* meaning "true, genuine" in Old High German). This is a kind of imitation. On the style of the preface and the identification of Erkambald as (Arch-) Bishop of Mainz, Strasbourg or Eichstätt, see the introduction.

10 *care*: this line has been interpreted in various ways, implying either that Gerald wrote for a long time, or with great efforts, or that he selected it from the many things (books?) in his care (e.g., Genzmer 1953 and Smyser & Magoun 1941). The crucial element is *de larga cura*. As Bate (1978: 52) remarks, this and the reference to "shortening the long day" in line 20, which implies only that the work is a way of passing the time, have been used to establish that Gerald is an old man, and hence not the author who describes

NOTES

himself at the end of the poem as being young.

11   *Gerald*: on the problems of his identity and authorship, see the introduction. He is clearly a German-speaker (Bate 1978: 4). Bate's comment on *fragilis* and the Germanic meaning of Gerald's name is a little far-fetched (1978: 53).

13   *Thunderer*: the Latin has *omnitonantem*, "all-thundering," and the poet might have had the biblical Boanerges in mind. Emendation to *omnitenentem*, "all-possessing," has been entertained, though most editors (including Kratz 1984, Wieland 1986, and Ring 2016) preserve the manuscript reading.

22   *brother*: *adelphus*, not the more usual monastic *frater*.

WALTHARIUS

1   *Europe*: the division of the world into three is a standard geographical point in the early middle ages, and later on the poet uses equally standard geographical definers for the western and eastern limits of Europe (see notes to line 1132). The address this time is to *fratres*, monastic brothers.

4   *Pannonia*: now Hungary, the Roman province was invaded by the Goths and the Lombards, and settled by the Avars in the sixth century, well after Attila's death, and later by the Magyars (Wallace-Hadrill 1967: 79).

11   *Attila*: historical ruler of the Huns, *Hunni*, here synonymous with the Avars, *Avares*, even though they are not the same. The threat of the Avars was closer in time, however. Attila, known as Etzel in Middle High German and Atli in Old Norse sources, is familiar in Germanic material, often in association with the equivalents of Gundahari and Hagano (see Gillespie under "Etzel"). He died in 453,

of a haemorrhage on his wedding-night to a princess with a Germanic name (Hildiko); one tradition has it that he was drunk. He led a number of attacks on the Eastern Roman Empire, and several sorties into Roman Gaul and Italy. He was defeated in 451 by the Roman Aetius and the Burgundians, Visigoths, and others in Gaul; see Schütte (1986: 72). The entry on Attila in the *Oxford Classical Dictionary*, edited by N. G. L. Hammond and H. H. Scullard (Oxford: Clarendon, 1973) concludes: "He was of a blustering, arrogant character, a persistent negotiator, but not pitiless." His setting up of treaties to build up an imperial power that failed after his death, so that the Huns eventually fade from the story, is a reflection—of sorts—of Attila's historical role. On the depiction of Attila in medieval Germanic literature, see de Boor (1963) and Neidorf (2023).

14   *Gibicho*: here the father of Gundahari, and king of the Franks. Gundahari, however, was historically King of the Burgundians (see note to line 34), and Gibica appears at the head of an ancestral list of Burgundian kings (see Gillespie under "Gibeche," the name he has in medieval German literature). The Franks ultimately absorbed the Burgundians (Wallace-Hadrill 1967: 64-114). Münkler (1983) links Gundahari with the Vandal king Gunderich, against whom the Visigoth Walja, a possible prototype for Walthari, fought.

27   *Hagano*: at least two figures bear this name in medieval Germanic writings, one in the *Nibelungenlied*, the other in *Kudrun*. The character in *Waltharius* is presumably the former (who dies in conflicts against Attila in German and Old Norse sources), though he is here made into a Frank, rather than a vassal of the Burgundians. The name links with "hawthorn" (Gillespie: "Hagene, 1" and also in his article [1965: 18]). The link with Troy recalls his name in the *Nibelungenlied*, "von Tronege Hagen," which has been discussed in detail by Grégoire (1934: 11-22), who takes it as Tongres, and there are several alternatives. Bate (1978: 54) points out that European royalty often claimed descent from the Trojans, and the Trojan warrior Pandarus

also appears later as an ancestor (of Werinhart). Bate also accepts the identification by Grégoire (1936: 212) of Hagen with Goar, a ruler of the Alans, another Germanic tribe, at the beginning of the fifth century, his name coming from the title *khagan*, "khan." Goar was apparently allied with Gundahari the Burgundian. Correct or not, the identification tells us very little. His father is named as Hagathio in line 629, and there is a play upon "hawthorn" at the end.

34 *Burgundians*: this Germanic group moved south-west to the Rhineland early in the fifth century. In 435-7, they were defeated and their king, Gundahari, killed by an army of Huns, brought in by Flavius Aetius, the Roman Governor of Gaul, after which the survivors moved to southern Gaul. These assisted Aetius in the defeat of the Huns under Attila in 451 (see note to line 11). Historically, the Burgundians (whose language appears to have been maintained until the seventh century) were given a set of laws in 516 by Gundobad, in which the names of Gibica and Gundahari appear. The Burgundians in southern Gaul were eventually absorbed by the Franks (see Gillespie under "Burgonde"). Gundahari appears as Gunther, a king ruling in Worms, in the *Nibelungenlied*, and in that work he is eventually destroyed by the Huns under Attila. See Gillespie under "Gunther, 1." Here, however, Gundahari has—presumably because Worms was at the time of the poem Frankish—become a Frank (although he is still in his historical role as a loser). Heririk (Heriricus) cannot be identified. The name appears in *Beowulf* (l. 2206), where the Geatish king Heardred is said to be the "nephew of Hereric"—whether this Hereric, who is evidently the brother of Hygd, Hygelac's wife, can be identified with the father of Hildigunda is unclear. Hildigunda (whose name appears awkwardly in Latin as Hiltgunt) might echo Hildiko, whom Attila married, dying the same night. Hildigunda here does cause some harm to Attila, of course: see Grégoire (1936: 211), though speculation on what might have been in a saga that might or might not have existed is less than productive. For a recent discussion of the idea that Hildigunda evolved out of Hildiko, see

Beckmann (2010: 91-107).

39   *Huns*: the text at this point refers to the Avars (the line has been broken to steal a few syllables for line 40, in which the name actually occurs). The Huns who settled Pannonia in the fourth and fifth centuries came from Asia, as did their successors in the region, the Avars in the sixth and the Magyars in the ninth, both of whom posed a similar threat in military terms to the Germanic tribes, and all of whom are confused with one another. Here and elsewhere "Hun" and "Avar" as indeed "gens Pannoniae" are completely interchangeable. See Gillespie under "Hiunen." The French *Chanson de Roland* (ll. 3241-54) has Huns, Avars, and presumably Magyars all lined up against the Franks.

52   *Chalon*: on the Saone. The Saone valley (and present-day Burgundy) was associated with the Burgundians by the time of the poem, just as the Franks were associated with the old Burgundian capital at Worms.

76   *Alphari*: ruler of Aquitania in the story, which in the period of Attila and Gundahari was a Visigoth kingdom (later taken over by the Franks). The name has been adapted slightly to make it match his son's, at least in the suffix. See line 839 on the name Alphari again. Gillespie (under "Walther") describes in detail the role played by the Walthari figure and his location in Spain or France, and notes that the association with the Vosges at the end might be linked with the settlement of the Basques in Aquitania (Aquitania being glossed as *uuasconolant* and the Vosges rendered in Middle High German as *Waskenwalt*). Grégoire (1936: 212 ff.) links Walthari with the Visigoth king Alaric as a model, but more specifically with a Visigoth king Wallia (Walja), ruling at Toulouse in the first decades of the fifth century. Grégoire sees the defeat of the supposed Franks at the hand of Walthari in the Vosges as a kind of poetic revenge for the battle of Vouillé in 507, when the Visigoth King of Aquitaine was defeated

and killed by Clovis the Merovingian Frank: but this is an historian's fancy. Münkler (1983: 46-56) also relates Walther and Aquitaine to the Visigoth kingdom and to Walja, giving fuller documentation, but apparently unaware that Grégoire had already made the point in 1936. The figure of Gualt(i)er del Hum (perhaps Walther from the Land of the Huns?) in the *Chanson de Roland* might echo our Walthari (see Heintze 1986; Millet 1995; Beckmann 2010), and the influence of *Waltharius* on the *Chanson de Roland* has been postulated: see de Vries (1963: 29). On the other versions of the story of Walthari and Hildigunda, see the introduction.

123   *Ospirina*: in the text Attila's queen is called Ospirin, and she matches no known figure, although Attila presumably had several wives and concubines, either in sequence or at one time. She has been given here a more feminine-looking name. Elsewhere in medieval Germanic literature, the name of Attila's wife is often Helche or Herche (see Gillespie, "Helche").

229   *betrothal*: see the extensive note by Bate (1978: 56-7) on the nature of the betrothal in the poem, which is Christian, in that Hildigunda clearly remains chaste until after the marriage (which is in any case after the end of the poem). Westra (1980), in an insightful reading of lines 215-59, perceives a betrothal ritual in this scene, with parallels in a bridal-quest narrative in Paul the Deacon's *Historia Langobardorum*. Bornholdt (2005: 42-85) regards this scene as perhaps the clearest indicator that the Walther story is connected to the Germanic bridal-quest tradition, where many elements in this scene find striking parallels.

264   *Smiths*: Strecker (1951: 35) reasonably supposes that the smith (actually "smiths," *fabrorum*) referred to here is Wayland, the archetypal smith and super-technician in the age of heroes, so greatly valued that he is kidnapped by a king in the Old Norse *Vǫlundarkviða*. Wayland is mentioned by name in line 965 in connection with

Walthari's armor (*Wielandia fabrica*). Ziolkowski (2001: 36-8) observes that the word *faber* and its derivatives are associated with Wayland elsewhere.

266 *Arm-rings*: the *armillas* which play such a vital part in the plot of *Waltharius* are gold torques or arm-rings, made perhaps of Roman imperial gold bullion. One is offered as a gift in the Old High German *Hildebrandslied*. Münkler (1983) discusses their great importance. For some illustrations, see Kent & Painter (1977).

327 *Lion*: this horse, presumably a heavy battle-charger given the amount it is expected to carry, is called *Leo* ("Lion") in Latin, a name which is rendered literally here, but might also be rendered as "Lionheart" in English. It is clearly valuable, since Gundahari claims in line 601 the treasure, the horse, and finally the girl.

333 *giant*: The suggestion that Walthari, in his armor, resembles a "giant" (Latin *gigans*) recalls passages in *Beowulf* in which it is suggested that the protagonist is stronger and larger than any ordinary mortal of his time (ll. 194-98a, ll. 247b-51a). Even if giants are elsewhere viewed negatively, the immediate context of this passage provides no reason to believe, as Ring (2016: 172) does, that there are "negative implications" in the poet's brief likening of the hero to a giant.

337 *in the fashion of the Huns*: to fight with two swords seems to have been known. There is evidence in the Old English *Waldere* that two swords are involved.

348 *Sun-God*: the text has *Phoebus*, this forming part of the somewhat convoluted manner of indicating the passing of time used elsewhere (line 428, for example). Strecker's notes make clear the Vergilian echoes (here referring to the *Georgics*).

NOTES

380 *king*: Bate (1978: 58) points out that the description of Attila's mood (though it is no longer strictly his hangover, in fact), echoes Dido's love-sickness for Aeneas in Vergil's *Aeneid*, although Aeneas' own worries in *Aeneid* VIII are not dissimilar. Attila's extreme reaction is also similar to that of the typical father in German bridal-quest narratives (e.g., *Ortnit* and *King Rother*) after he loses control of his daughter. Additionally, in *The Klage*, Attila is depicted as an extremely emotional figure; he is rebuked there by Dietrich von Bern for his excessive mourning (Neidorf 2023: 1324-8).

407 *I live*: the Latin is not entirely clear. As Strecker (1951: 41) and Bate (1978: 58) note, the scansion demands a short final -o, so that the whole seems to mean "as I live" (abbreviated for *si vivo*) rather than "to the living man," though in spite of Bate, that does make sense, and royal promises of reward often carry the proviso that the claimant has to survive. In this case, none of the warriors to whom this is offered wants to take the risk.

427 *decently*: Walthari exhibits the chastity of a Christian warrior.

433 *Worms*: the traditional Burgundian capital, here ruled over by the right king but of the wrong people, though by the time of *Waltharius* it was in Frankish hands, of course.

434 *fish*: it is not quite clear where Walthari caught this fish if it was outside Gundahari's lands (or indeed when he did so, which in culinary terms might be more to the point). The geography is not particularly realistic, however. At all events, it is interesting to have a fish as a recognition token, rather than, say, a ring or a key found inside one. Perhaps this is evidence for free composition on the poet's part or evidence for the influence of non-heroic narrative traditions upon the poem.

475 *twelve*: parallels with the disciples, but also with the twelve peers

of the *Chanson de Roland* or the twelve retainers of the protagonist in *Beowulf* come to mind.

483 *Frankish treasure*: Gundahari, though consistently depicted in a negative manner in this poem (Kratz 1980: 33-7; Scherello 1986), offers here a legal justification for his assault on Walther, namely, that Walther is traveling with the treasure that Gibicho, Gundahari's father, had given in tribute to Attila. On the legal and ethical dimensions of the poem, and their potential contemporary resonances, see Stone (2013) and MacLean (2018).

490 *Vosges*: a certain amount of geographical freedom is required for a route from the land of the Huns via Worms to Aquitaine (Gillespie 1973: 137). See the note to line 76.

545 *cut my throat*: in the apocryphal *Vita Adae et Evae*, Eve asks Adam to kill her when they have been ejected from paradise. He refuses in similar terms to those used by Walthari.

555 *Nibelungs*: in the Latin the word is *nebulones*, and much discussed. As Bate (1978: 59-60) notes, citing Grégoire (1934), "it would be very surprising if Nibelung Franks were not being referred to." Bate and Ring (2016: 177) discuss the possible puns on "rogues" and on "dust" (see also Ziolkowski 2001: 45).

566 *forgiveness*: Bate (1978: 60) sees this as an extreme example of parody. It recalls, however, the scene in the *Chanson de Roland* in which Roland asks for a kind of blanket forgiveness before going into his last battle.

581 *Kamalo*: as governor of Metz, he is clearly a vassal of Gundahari (who can therefore send him out as messenger, not always a very safe task). The name is probably related to OHG *gamal*, meaning "old." Bate (1978: 60) notes the possibility of a connection with Ortwin of

Metz, who is said in the *Nibelungenlied* to be the nephew of Hagen (a role assigned in *Waltharius* to Patafrid). In addition to Bate's observation, it is interesting to note that in the Vienna fragment of the Middle High German poem on *Walther and Hildegund* (Learned 1892: 67-72; Magoun & Smyser 1950: 42-7), Ortwin of Metz is mentioned as a hostile character who would have obstructed Walther's journey home if encountered along the way.

621 *dream*: prophetic dreams are common in heroic poetry, though this is specific. There is a later reference to a bear. It is reminiscent of the dreams of Charlemagne in the *Chanson de Roland* (ll. 725-36). Other potential parallels to Hagen's dream include the dream of Kriemhilt in the *Nibelungenlied* and certain episodes in the bridal-quest tradition (Bornholdt 2005: 1, 51, 157).

629 *Hagathio*: Hagen's parentage varies in different works—in the *Nibelungenlied*, for instance, Hagen's father is named Aldrian—and this is the only extant reference to Hagathio. Bate (1978: 60-61) comments that he has been linked with the Roman Aetius.

652 This line, which repeats line 647, is not actually printed by Strecker, but he notes that it appears in the margin in the manuscript followed; it is not clear why he does not print it, and Bate omits it, considering it to be just a gloss on what is being said in the text, so that his line-numbers are one out from that point against Strecker. Some translators have left it out, others have included it, and we have chosen to do the latter.

668 *thick*: the Latin has *triplicem clipeum*, literally "three-ply," probably with layers of leather.

674 *Amazingly*: possibly too modern a version for *ecce*, although the vividly described incident is startling. It is recounted largely in a vivid present tense, which sounds somewhat odd in English. Smyser

& Magoun (1941) try to imitate the tenses, and the result is a somewhat curious mixture at times.

683   *leg*: the Latin is not entirely clear, and we follow Strecker (1951) in explanation of what is happening in this fast scene.

686   *nephew*: The uncle-nephew relationship is common in Germanic writing (often however—as with Patafrid—it is a *sister's* son). Charlemagne and Roland in the *Chanson* are probably the best known example; Hygelac and Beowulf are another. The passage is not entirely clear and Bate (1978: 61) takes *Kimo* as being in apposition to *filius*; Gillespie ("Kimo") also sees Skaramund as a byname. It makes sense, however, to take Kimo as the brother, and we have followed Strecker. As Gillespie points out, however, Scaramundus is recorded as a family name. Neither name has other associations.

698   *helmet*: the plumes are actually a horse's tail.

713   *helmet*: the combination of noise and sparks from swords (or in this case pommels) against helmets is a stock feature of Germanic battle-scenes, with plenty of illustrations of the point in *Kudrun*, for example.

720   *proud*: the epithet *superbus* is regularly applied to Gundahari, and the translation is necessarily inadequate.

725   *Werinhart*: another German name, again without particular associations elsewhere. However, the poet has him descended from Pandarus, the Trojan archer, who in the *Iliad* is urged by Athena to fire an arrow at Menelaus and thus break the truce. This is referred to in the *Aeneid*, and the passage provides a very clear example of the many direct borrowings from Vergil. The passage in the *Aeneid* (V. 495-97) reads:

> Tertius Eurytion, tuus, o clarissime, frater,
> Pandare, qui quondam iussus confundere foedus
> In medios telum torsisti primus Achivos...

and our text:

> Tertius en Werinhardus abit bellumque lacessit,
> ...
> O vir clare, tuus cognatus et artis amator
> Pandare, qui quondam iussus confundere foedus
> In medios telum torsisti primus Achivos

and there are other echoes in the same passage. The passage in the *Aeneid* occurs during the funeral games, however, and note that Eurytion is the brother of Pandarus; Werinhart, much later, is a descendant of a Trojan warrior, like Hagano. Strecker (1951) points out the parallel with Vergil in his exhaustive notes, and it is a clear example. But Strecker also lists the phrase *arcum pharetramque*, "bow and quiver," in Prudentius's *Psychomachia* in relation to the reference to Werinhart's weapons. The match is not identical, and it is difficult to think of an alternative in Latin for bow and arrow. As has been pointed out, Strecker (1951) can be a little *too* exhaustive at times in its notes. Werinhart has had a well-established place in *Waltharius* scholarship—his episode receives chapter-length attention in Ebeling-Koning's study (1977: 21-98), for instance—but the reader will search in vain for this character in Ring's edition (2016), where his name is given as Ewarhardus (Evarhart) on the basis of certain manuscript variants. For our part, it seemed best to preserve the traditional name of this character (and others) if for no other reason than to facilitate comprehension of the poem's critical literature.

756 *Ekifrid*: Ekivrid in the text, he is possibly linked with the character named Irnfrit in the *Nibelungenlied* (Gillespie, "Hadawardus"). Ekifrid is an outlaw on the run for killing a nobleman; a similar

situation is ascribed to Ecgtheow, the father of the protagonist, in *Beowulf*. Ekifrid is described as a Saxon, but it has been suggested that he is actually an Anglo-Saxon (hence his link with the Celtic world—see note on line 765) and we find the idea credible, without going so far as to give him the Old English name *Ecgfrið*. His horse is actually a chestnut with different flecks, and recalls Ganelon's horse in the *Chanson de Roland* –'Tachebrun' ('Brown-spots'). Ring (2016) changes Ekifrid's name to Ekerich, though the distribution of manuscript variants does not appear to support such a reading.

763   *wood-demon*: Bate (1978) notes that the passage contains puns, but they are impossible to imitate. The play is on *saltus*, "woods, wooded hills," in which the supposed demon is at home, and *walt-* and *her* in German as parts of the hero's name (though not necessarily in its *Walthari* form): see Morgan (1972) on the whole passage, including the *Celtica lingua* reference, and note to line 774.

765   *Celtic tongue*: this is one of the most frequently debated passages of the text. The line reads: "Celtica lingua probat te ex illa gente creatum..." and the first two words, literally "[Your] Celtic speech..." have been taken as meaning "nonsense, double-Dutch" by Strecker (1951: 55). The curious "Irish brogue (Low German speech)" in Smyser & Magoun (1941: 129) seems to imply that Walthari misinterprets the Saxon accent. Bate (1978: 61-2) stretches interpretation somewhat in assuming Ekifrid to be a (by definition illegitimate) son of a Saxon mother and an itinerant Irish cleric, which seems harder on Ekifrid than necessary. If we take him as an Anglo-Saxon, he can be linked more easily with the other people of the British Isles. The reading of *celticus* as "nonsensical" is probably correct. For further discussion of the implications of this phrase, see Jones (1974) and Dumville (1983).

774   *wooden*: Morgan (1972) notes the continuation of the puns on woodmen, *wald*, and Walthari with the verb *transponit*, to plant a tree.

NOTES

We have tried to match this with a rather different pun.

781 *Hadawart*: Perhaps linked with Hawart of the *Nibelungenlied* (Gillespie 1973: 56), who is connected to Irnfrit (the Ekifrid of *Waltharius*?) in that text.

794 *poison*: poisoned arrows were outlawed in Germanic custom (Genzmer 1953: 61).

797 *arrows*: the Latin has just *telum*, projectile, but the point made is that Hadawart fights close in, not at a distance, as the others have so far done.

839 *Alphari's son*: the Latin uses the Vergilian patronymic *Alpharides* to denote Walthari here and elsewhere, just as *Pandarides* is used in line 737 for Werinhart.

846 *Patafrid*: the name is rare (see Gillespie, "Patavrid"). Patafrid again shows the nephew relationship, this time to Hagano in the classic sister's son form. The relationship will be invoked again later. Although there are Vergilian echoes in Hagano's failed attempt to persuade him not to fight, and cases in which a warrior takes on an opponent who outclasses him (*viribus impar*) are not uncommon, the passage demonstrates considerable skill. Many critics have, however, expressed the view that Hagano's "whirlpool of avarice" speech is somewhat out of place in an heroic epic, and contrasts somewhat with the main aim of the whole exercise, which is to take the Hunnish gold from Walthari. Strecker (1951) provides no parallels for the image of Death grinning at the doomed Patafrid, although it sounds homiletic (*aspice mortem/ Qualiter arridet!*). For an insightful discussion of the classical resonances in the Patafrid episode, see Flatt (2016: 476-80). Neidorf (2021: 829-33) observes that the figure of Patafrid is comparable to other impetuous young men who refuse to be dissuaded and force a reluctant adversary to kill them; clear

examples of this character type include Hlǫð in *Hlǫðskviða*, Hadubrand in the *Hildebrandslied*, and Garulf in the *Finnsburg Fragment*.

886 *slaughterer*: a fairly free version of *tyrannus*, which has a variety of meanings.

888 *rugged*: the Latin actually has *nodosus*, "knotty," though it is unclear what effect this has on the nature of the spear.

893 *heartbeat*: the Latin reads literally "when the thin blood had returned to her heart." The sense is clear, however.

900 *attack*: Strecker (1951) sees Patafrid as being on horseback, although this is not always apparent. We hear later (lines 1170 ff.) of eleven horses (six kept by Walthari, two dead and three driven off by the king), so that presumably all the warriors ride in. Walthari, of course, is not fighting on horseback.

914 *Gerwit*: not otherwise known. We are told later, in line 940 that he had been an Earl (*comes*, "Count") in the city of Worms, close therefore to Gundahari. The text does not explain why he specifically moves in to avenge Patafrid.

933 *tire*: it is not entirely clear what Gerwit is doing, but he seems to be trying to make Walthari, who is on foot, keep up with him. The Latin is ambiguous: see Strecker's (1951) notes on *fatigatum*, and Bate (1978) on the unusual form *homonem*, which occurs also in line 578. Smyser & Magoun (1941) consider that Gerwit is trying to escape, although *fallere* [*fallare*] is unlikely to mean this.

938 *died*: not specifically present, but justified by the sense.

962 *Randolf*: once again a name not known elsewhere in medieval Germanic literature.

965 *Wayland*: the legendary smith probably implied, but not named, in line 264 (admittedly a plural there). The Old English fragment of *Waldere* contains the phrase *Welandes worc* (l. 2), which refers to a sword, rather than armor, but looks like our *Wielandia fabrica*. A nearly identical phrase, *Welandes geweorc*, appears twice in *Beowulf* (ll. 406, 455). Wayland's productions are found elsewhere in Germanic writings: in addition to Beowulf's sword and armor, the sword Mimminc (Mimungr etc.), which plays an important role in *Þiðreks saga*, is made by Wayland. On the possibility that oral formulae from vernacular tradition, such as *Welandes worc*, have informed the composition of *Waltharius*, see Olsen (1993). For a wide-ranging discussion of arms and armor in the poem, see Ziolkowski (2008). Kratz (1984: 204) remarks that "Wayland or Wieland in Norse mythology is the god of smiths," but that is not quite accurate. Extant sources vaguely associate Wayland with the supernatural (he is called the "lord of elves" in *Vǫlundarkviða*), but they neither state nor imply that he is a god, much less a god of smiths.

982 *Helmnot*: this time the name appears elsewhere in Germanic writings (see Gillespie 1973: 67), but this man has a cognomen (line 1008)—Eleuthir, an interesting Greek name (*eleutheros*, "freeman"). Bate (1978: 63) points out that the poet provides the name with a Greek termination in line 1017, and his method of fighting, with a trident, sounds more classical than Germanic.

995 *Enough*: in the Latin *Quid moror?* "Why delay?"—a nice and perhaps self-ironic touch after a somewhat far-fetched image.

1008 *Eleuthir* etc.: the action is speeding up as Walthari now has to tackle four against one (and note that Hagano is still distanced from the fray). Drogo (a more familiar version than Latin *Trogus*) is from Strasbourg (*Argentina* in Latin, also *Argentoratum*, then in Frankish hands and the scene of the famous Oaths between the Carolingian brothers in 842). Tanasto is from Speyer in the Rhineland, but his name is difficult to link with anything, and its etymology is uncertain (Gillespie, "Tanastus"). His name has been adapted slightly so that he looks less like a Latin interloper. These are the tenth and eleventh men, and Gundahari makes up the twelfth by joining in the fight at this point, though he himself called for twelve to ride with him, and the twelfth is actually Hagano, who is here excluded.

1017   *Helmnot*: the text uses his other name, in Greek form (*Eleuthrin*), at this point, but the double name can be confusing.

1037   *copper-banded*: our invention (moved to the next line). The text speaks of a green (*viridis*) sheath, which might be dyed leather. It might also have old copper or bronze fittings, gone green with age.

1059   *neck*: the line actually says "put the gold collar round his neck" and it has been much debated. Gold is red in medieval writing, not yellow, and Walthari has cut off the heads of the other fallen in a regular, if barbaric, gesture. Strecker (1951) comments on various possibilities in his notes, and also points out that Walthari is not actually victorious yet, since the king is armed, and still on his feet, although he does not stay for long.

1061   *heels*: this presumably means that the bodies are twitching spasmodically; one is headless and the other dismembered, after all.

1062   *Gundahari*: it should be noted that while every one of his warriors stands his ground and fights to the death, Gundahari is the only one who, having already engaged the enemy, runs away.

1066 ff.   *Hagano*: Hagano's ironic speech is witty and makes its point perfectly clearly, building upon the aspersion cast upon Hagathio in line 630. Once again, Hagano has the best parts of dialogue.

NOTES

1082   *king*: Gundahari actually refers to himself as *orbis caput*, "chief of the world." Walthari is referred to as *tyrannus*.

1094   *blushed*: *Erubuit domini vultum* in the text; *erubuscere vultum* means "to blush," and certainly Hagano is thinking about his honor at this point (although he has a lot of argument left). Smyser & Magoun (1941) translate as "he had regard for his lord," agreeing with the note in Strecker (1951), which refers to the use of a similar construction (perhaps behind the phrase?) in the Vulgate IV Reg. iii (King James Version II Kings iii: 14) translated as "had regard for" both in the Douay and the Authorised Versions. The poet may be thinking in biblical terms here, since—as Strecker notes—the question "where shall I follow you, O lord?" (line 1098) may also have biblical or liturgical origins.

1120   *behind*: Bate (1978: 64) notes that after Hagano's speech to Gundahari, the proposed plan of attacking Walthari from behind, two against one, is not particularly heroic.

1132   *Spain*: at the time of the poem, the standard geographical works (especially Isidore of Seville's *Etymologies*, a much read encyclopaedia, and works by Orosius and others) took as limitations to the west either *ultima Thule* (which remains a famous tag, meaning Iceland), Ireland, or Gades (Cadiz) and the Pillars of Hercules. These are the limits of Europe (and we recall the geographical opening, line 1). They would be the last to be touched by the setting sun, described here as *Phoebus* in classical fashion. That the poet has the standard geographies in mind is clear later when the sunrise begins in the eastern limit, the island of Taprobane (Ceylon), which overlapped largely with India for the medieval geographer (see line 1189). Early medieval works frequently see Europe as extending from the tip of Spain to Ceylon, and from Ethiopia to the Rhipaean Mountains, a northern range which became increasingly arctic as known geography becomes more advanced. The Latin of 1132 actually refers to "the Irish" and "the Spanish."

1134   *Evening Star*: *Hesperos* (or *Hesperus*) usually refers to the Evening Star, though the text is difficult to interpret here; Smyser & Magoun (1941) make it refer to the moon.

1156   *hawthorn*: *paliurus* is clearly used as a pun on the interpretation of Hagano's name (*Hagedorn*, "hawthorn"), as there are several references to thorns, and the pun is made explicit later in line 1351.

1171   *king*: usually the Latin refers to the king as Guntharius, though here he is named for the sole time in German, as *rex Gunthere*, the form his name would have at the period of the poem. We have of course adopted elsewhere a deliberately archaic form. The total of eleven horses implies that all the battles began with the attacker mounted. The king and the last two companions were presumably not on horseback during the rope-pulling attempt, and Gundahari mounted quickly to escape, so that the other two horses may be assumed to be those of Drogo and Tanasto.

1188   *Daystar*: the text has *Lucifer*, the morning star ("son of the morning" in Isaiah XIV), and the announcement is in direct speech (*dicens*). We have adapted somewhat the description of the sunrise in line 1189, which actually says: "the island of Taprobane sees the bright sun." However, as indicated in the notes to lines 1130ff., the poet is simply using standard geographical references for west and east. Taprobane means Ceylon (the encyclopaedias usually comment simply that elephants come from there), but there is a strong overlap with India, as a glance at any of the medieval *mappae mundi* makes clear, and to the modern English mind, the "great country in the east where the sun rises" would connote India rather than Ceylon (Sri Lanka, Serendip, and so on), if indeed a country would be named at all.

NOTES

1196 *sixth*: as we hear a little later (line 1206), his own horse is still carrying the chests of gold taken from the Huns, and Walthari, now mounted, leads it.

1232 *rabid*: literally, "gnashing with rabid teeth," a slightly odd formulation in English (as in Smyser & Magoun 1941)

1233 *dare*: actually *si vis*, "if you will." We have strengthened various elements of Gundahari's speech.

1235 *Fortune*: *Fortuna*—a somewhat obscure passage, literally something like "you have purchased Fortuna."

1272 *flower*: a reference to Patafrid, in spite of what Hagano has said earlier in line 1112.

1285 *second hour*: Smyser & Magoun (1941) estimate 5:30 a.m., but "the sixth hour" is sometimes interpreted as noon, so that this could be a little later than they suggest.

1287 *wicked*: a problematic passage. The Latin text has *maligeram*, which might mean "evil-bearing"; an alternative suggestion (based on a reading in some of the manuscripts) is *maligenam*, meaning "made of apple-wood." Spears sometimes have such descriptions attached to them (e.g., *fraxineum*, "of ash-wood," is in line 1295 and *nodosus*, "knotty," is used earlier). However, a reading with the sense of "wicked" is satisfying in the context. Bate (1978: 65) points out that there are problems with the meter. A late manuscript has the reading *malignam*, "evil."

1288 *Walthari*: he is not named in this line, but in line 1290 as *Alpharides*. However, we have had to recast the passage and rearrange the lines, which in Latin place the object (the spear) at the beginning, a construction which would be awkward in English.

1294 *stuck*: the Latin is graphic, and the spear sticks into the ground *usque ad clavos*, "right down to the nails which pin the iron head to the wooden shaft."

1320 *once*: the Latin does not contain what is here included as a parenthetic anticipatory indication "as we shall hear," but the text reads rather oddly without a pointer of some kind; the single exceptional occasion referred to when Walthari drops his extreme caution is presumably (as Smyser & Magoun 1941 indicate) in lines 1381-3, when Hagano is able to cut off Walthari's hand.

1337 *Numidian bear*: the Vergilian image appears to be based on the passage in the *Aeneid* X (ll. 707-13) in which Mezentius fights like a boar held at bay by snapping hounds (Strecker 1951). The opening formula *Haud aliter* "not unlike..." is typical. Numidia is in North Africa. The Molossi are a tribe in northern Greece/Sparta, but fierce Molossian hounds figure regularly in classical writing (e.g., *Georgics* III. 405, but closer to our passage is Horace's *Epodes* VI. 5).

1343 *after noon*: literally "at the ninth hour"; they have been fighting, of course, since the second hour (line 1285).

1351 *Hawthorn*: the resolution of the pun on Hagano's name (modern German *Hagedorn*) already indicated. The line contains the word *vires*, a verbal form meaning "you grow green," but which recalls the noun *vires*, "strength," in line 1350 (Bate 1978: 65). It is worth noting that Stecker (1951: 79) is critical of Grégoire's comments on Hagen and the hawthorn-pun.

1357 *struck*: actually "weighs down" or "burdens" (*onerat*). Presumably the spear goes through the leather and wood of the shield, out sufficiently to damage Hagano's body-armor, but not enough—since he is well-protected all round—to cause more than a slight (*modicum*) flesh-wound.

1376 *shattered sword*: commenting on the breaking of Walthari's sword, Kratz (1984: 204) asserts that the passage "alludes to scenes in the *Aeneid* and *Psychomachia*" and that "[n]either reference is flattering to Walter." It should be noted, however, that scenes in which swords break or fail also occur in medieval Germanic literature (e.g., *Beowulf*), and they do not reflect negatively on the hero there. The argument of Kratz's monograph (1980), echoed frequently in the commentary of Ring (2016), that classical allusions often serve to communicate subliminal criticisms of Walthari does not appear persuasive to us. For a thoughtful critique of Kratz's method, see the review by Ziolkowski (1983).

1395 *twice three*: the use of *bis ternos...molares* presumably means that Hagano lost upper and lower back teeth. Bate (1978: 66-7) discusses in detail the various losses—a hand, a leg, and the eye and teeth, of which we are graphically reminded in the lines that follow. He links these all with the biblical passages of Matthew V. 29 ff., Matthew XVIII. 7-9 and 20, and Mark IX. 42-6; he notes that there is reference there to a right eye and to a right hand, but that which foot is to be cut off (as in Mark IX. 44) is not specified, as here (see also Kratz 1980: 50-2; Ring 2016: 189-91). It is hardly necessary to comment that the poet was as aware as we are that the wounds (and probably Hagano's above all) would hardly permit of jovial banter immediately after. The ending is scarcely realistic. Since there are no references to the three characters with these wounds elsewhere in Germanic writings, it is reasonable to suppose that the biblical passages helped to form the text, although from all that has happened so far, one might have expected, were this a Germanic heroic poem (whether or not such a version ever actually existed), a tragic ending in which Walthari killed Gundahari, thus forcing Hagano, his friend, to kill him. Instead, we have a biblically-tinged and (not just for the modern reader) faintly ludicrous set of mutilations and a happy ending of sorts, which looks like an avoidance of a final sequence of deaths and broken loyalties all turning on the spoils of Attila's treasure-house. A tragic ending has probably been avoided (rather than changed). But not every Germanic heroic epic ends in tragedy in any case; the *Nibelungenlied* may have a tragic outcome, but *Kudrun* does not. The connections between the Walther legend and the bridal-quest tradition, observed most comprehensively by Bornholdt (2005: 42-85), lend support to the notion that the Walther legend originally featured a happy ending, involving homecoming and marriage, even if that ending were not precisely the same as the one in *Waltharius*. For additional considerations against the hypothesis that the story originally featured a tragic ending, see Dronke (1977: 31-32) and Flatt (2016: 482-5).

1421   *Thorny*: the adjective from the pun has now become a kind of attributive. Walthari is again described as "the man from Aquitaine."

1429   *Mind you*: the Latin line opens with the word *Wah*, providing the translator with a range of possibilities depending upon register, but it is less than usual in a Vergilian hexameter, and contrasts with the interjected *(h)eu(-ge)* a few lines later.

1434   *Walthari*: Strecker prints the name as *Walthare*, which as Stach (1943: 68) points out is a mixture of German and Latin; the earliest form would be Walthari, which would move to Waltheri, Walthere (thus in two manuscripts) and finally Walther.

1435   *Frank*: the Latin has *Sicamber*, a name of some antiquity. The Sicambri (the spelling varies) were an early Germanic tribe living on the Rhine and defeated by the Romans; eventually they became part of the Frankish federation, and the poet uses their name simply as a synonym for "Frank."

1450   *thirty years*: Bate (1978: 67) refers to the *Aeneid*, but the period

NOTES

mentioned is standard in other poetry as a period of long and presumably effective rule. We may recall that Beowulf, after the vigorous youth which forms the subject of much of the poem, rules wisely for fifty years. Note that Walthari has now publicly betrothed himself to Hildigunda. One of the Middle High German analogues, the Vienna fragment (Learned 1892: 67-72; Magoun & Smyser 1950: 42-7), depicts their homecoming and marriage preparations.

1455   *barely*: the Latin *nondum* "not yet" (which I interpret as "barely") need not apply only to the leaving of the nest, and translations vary. See Langosch (1956) for a different version, for example.

1456   *tale*: the term *poesis* usually means a long poem, *poema* usually a short one. This distinction cannot really be made in English, but "tale" and "song" seem to be rough equivalents.

Explicit: taken from the Brussels/Gembloux manuscript B, one of the earliest full texts.

APPENDIX
TWO LATIN BATTLE-POEMS

Probably composed within a century of *Waltharius*, these two poems deal with battles fought by some of the same peoples. The first shows the demise of the warriors of Pannonia, the second the breakdown of the group that eventually achieved hegemony in Europe, the Franks. Far closer to their actual events, both are historical poems, which means that they select and present with a bias appropriate to the individual poet. The first celebrates in theocentric fashion the Christianization of the Avars, and the second laments, quite properly, the internecine breakdown of Charlemagne's empire. The days of the heroes are past.

In the attempt to make these pieces into readably modern poems, the meter and language of the originals (the two poems are rather different) have been rendered by an irregular and loosely alliterative verse (which is not meant to imply that there was a German(ic) original for either). I have tried to imitate Angilbert's abecedarian pattern, though Helen Waddell chose not to in the rather different version in her *Medieval Latin Lyrics*.

1. THE END OF THE AVAR HUNS

The Avars, once a force in European history of massive importance, incorporating the White Huns and related to the Tartars, had settled in the Danube basin. Traditionally ruled by a khagan or khan and living in great ring-form camps, they fought against the Lombards and the Franks. Charlemagne himself fought against them from 788 onward, and eventually his son, Pepin (who predeceased him in the year 810, in spite of the pious hopes of this work), together with the Lombard Duke of Friuli, conquered them. They accepted Christianity, did homage to Charlemagne, and he reinstated a khagan over them. They were eventually to be displaced by another group, the Magyars, and all but forgotten by history. The poem was edited by Dümmler (1881: 116); it was previously translated by Godman (1985: 187-91).

2. ANGILBERT AT FONTENAILLES

On June 25, 841, near Auxerre, the three sons of the Holy Roman Emperor Louis the Pious (surviving brother of King Pepin, victor over the Avars) fought against each other: Charles, later King of the West Franks (roughly of modern France), and Ludwig of Bavaria (whose untranslated Germanic name reflects his kingship of the East Franks, roughly modern Germany) fought against the heir to the Empire, Lothar. Angilbert, the author of this poem, fought on Lothar's side, but Lothar was defeated, apparently let down by his own forces. In the following year, the other brothers confirmed their alliance in the Oaths of Strasbourg, and the Partition of Verdun in the next laid the basis for modern France, Germany, and a disputed *Lothari Regnum*—Lorraine—between the two. The battle of Fontanetum, Fontenay, Fontenoy, or Fontenailles is a crucial point in European history, comparable with the defeat of the Saracens at Poitiers by Charles Martel in 732 or the Battle of the Nations in 1813. That these scarcely figure in the Anglophone reader's general historical knowledge is telling; against them, Hastings, Bannockburn or Mafeking are of limited importance indeed, and it has been said that "the history of modern Europe is an exposition of the Treaty of Verdun" (which followed from this battle). Helen Waddell linked the horror expressed here with that of the battle-fields of France in 1916, not too far away. She also notes that the poem was well-known and was set to music. It is in Dümmler (1884: 137), as well as in Waddell (1952: 112-7) and Langosch (1968: 142-5). Nothing is known of the eye-witness poet. A more celebrated Angilbert was at Charlemagne's court with Alcuin, but he died in 814. For a recent discussion of the battle and the poem, see Flynn (2022). For arguments that *Waltharius* might have been composed in the aftermath of the battle, see Rio (2015) and Turcan-Verkerk (2016).

DE PIPPINI REGIS VICTORIA AVARICA

1. Omnes gentes qui fecisti, tu Christe, dei soboles,
terras, fontes, rivos, montes et formasti hominem,
Avaresque convertisti ultimis temporibus.

2. Multa mala iam fecerunt ab antico tempore,
fana dei destruxerunt atque monasteria,
vasa aurea sacrata, argentea, fictilia.

3. Vestem sanctam polluerunt de ara sacratissima,
linteamina levitae et sanctaemonialium
muliebribus tradata suadente demone.

4. Misit deus Petrum sanctum, principem apostolum,
in auxilium Pippini magni regis filium,
ut viam eius comitaret et Francorum aciem.

5. Rex accinctus dei virtute Pippin, rex catholicus,
castra figit super flumen albidum Danubium,
hostibus accingens totum undique praesidia.

6. Unguimeri satis pavens, Avarorum genere,
regi dicens satis forte: 'Tu Cacane perdite!'
atque Catunae mulieri, maledictae coniugi:

7. 'Regna vestra consumata, ultra non regnabitis,
regna vestra diu longe cristianis tradita,
a Pippino demollita, principe catholico.

TRANSLATION

KING PEPIN'S VICTORY OVER THE AVAR HUNS

All people that you made, O Lord, are offspring of God,
you made the lands, the rivers, shores and mountains, and then man;
and now at last the White Huns have been brought to You.

Since ancient times, the evil they have done is great,
destroyed God's temples, and the monasteries too,
and sacred vessels, be they gold or silver or of clay.

Laid wicked hands on holy vestments from High Altars
mocked those smooth and holy cloths, and gave
them, devil-driven, to their womenfolk.

God sent Saint Peter, Prince of the Apostles
to Pepin's aid, to help the great king's son,
to fight beside him and his Frankish force.

King Pepin, armed with the strength of God and Holy Church
pitched camp above the White Danube,
and ringed the enemy round with his troops.

The Hun Unguimer, greatly frightened,
cried out to his king, "Khan, you are lost,
you and Lady Katuna, ill-starred couple.

Your kingdom devoured, you will rule no more,
your lands will be held henceforth by the Christians
brought down by Pepin, the Catholic Prince.

8. Adpropinquat rex Pippinus forti cum exercitu,
fines tuos occupare, depopulare populum,
montes, silvas atque colles ponere presidia.

9. Tolle cito, porta tecum copiosa munera;
sceptrum regis adorare, ut paullum possis vivere,
aurum, gemmas illi offer, ne te tradat funeri.'

10. Audiens Cacanus rex, undique perterritus,
protinus ascendens mulam cum Tarcan primatibus,
regem venit adorare et plagare munere.

11. Regi dicens: 'Salve princeps, esto noster dominus,
regnum meum tibi trado cum festucis et foliis,
silvas, montes atque colles cum omnibus nascentiis.

12. Tolle tecum proles nostras, parent tibi obsequia,
de primatibus nec parcas, terga verte acie,
colla nostra, proles nostras dicioni tradimus.'

13. Nos fideles cristiani deo agamus gratiam,
qui regnum regis confirmavit super regnum Uniae,
et victoriam donavit de paganis gentibus.

14. Vivat, vivat rex Pippinus in timore domini,
avus regnet et senescat et procreet filios,
qui palatia conservent in vita et post obitum.

15. Qui conclusit regnum crande, amplum, potentissimum,
quae regna terrae non fecerunt usque ad diem actenus,
neque Cesar et pagani, sed divina gratia.

Gloria aeterna patri, gloria sit filio.

TRANSLATION

King Pepin approaches with his mighty army
to occupy your lands and kill your people,
take over all your hills and woods and mountains.

Open your gates, give treasures, gold,
accept his sovereignty, and you may survive,
offer him wealth and jewels, lest he destroy you."

The Khan heard and he trembled.
He and his Tartar nobles now saddled up and went
to submit to the king, and settle with tribute,

saying to the king: "Hail my lord prince. Accept our homage,
I render up my kingdom, root and branch,
its woods, mountains and hills, and all its men.

Take all our people; they bow before you
and if it please you, turn back your troops
from our lands. We give you all this freely."

We faithful Christians may give thanks to God
who strengthened our king's rule against the Huns
and gave him victory over the pagan forces.

Long may King Pepin live in the fear of the Lord,
may he live long, rule in age, and see his sons
confirm his kingdom in life and in posterity.

What makes a kingdom great, and gives it power over all,
what made the kingdoms of the earth, until the present day
is neither Caesar nor the pagans, but the grace of God.

Eternal glory to the Father and the Son.

VERSUS DE BELLA QUAE FUIT ACTA FONTANETO

1. Aurora cum primo mane tetram noctem dividet,
Sabbatum non illud fuit, sed Saturni dolium,
de fraterna rupta pace gaudet demon impius.

2. Bella clamat, hinc et inde pugna gravis oritur,
frater fratri mortem parat, nepoti avunculus;
filius nec patri suo exhibet quod meruit.

3. Caedes nulla peior fuit campo nec in Marcio;
fracta est lex christianorum sanguinis proluvio,
unde manus inferorum, gaudet gula Cerberi.

4. Dextera prepotens dei protexit Hlotharium,
victor ille manu sua pugnavitque fortiter:
ceteri si sic pugnassent, mox foret concordia.

5. Ecce olim velut Iudas salvatorem tradidit,
sic te, rex, tuique duces tradiderunt gladio:
esto cautus, ne frauderis agnus lupo previo.

6. Fontaneto fontem dicunt, villam quoque rustici,
ubi strages et ruina Francorum de sanguine:
orrent campi, orrent silvae, orrent ipsi paludes.

TRANSLATION

THE BATTLE FOUGHT AT FONTENAILLES

And dawn came. It divided day from night,
but brought no Holy Sabbath; it was heathen Saturn's hell-brew,
and the very devil delighting in discord between brothers.

Battle-noises. All around, fierce fighting begins,
as brother brings death to brother, uncle to nephew,
even son to father, defying all natural love.

Carnage and slaughter were never worse on the field of Mars,
the laws of Christ broken, blood shed like rain,
all down to hell, into the eager throat of Cerberus.

Divine protection, God's right hand on Lothar,
and his own strong arm let him strive boldly to victory;
had others proved as brave, peace would soon have come.

Even as Judas once betrayed our Savior,
so, Lord King, your princes led you to the sword.
Beware! The wolf in the fold will kill the lamb.

Fontenailles, named for a fountain, in farmland
is where the Frankish forces fell in blood and ruin,
making the woods and fields and marshland tremble.

7. Gramen illud ros et ymber nec humectat pluvia,
in quo fortes ceciderunt, proelio doctissimi,
pater, mater, soror, frater, quos amici fleverant.

8. Hoc autem scelus peractum, quod descripsi ritmice,
Angelbertus ego vidi pugnansque cum aliis,
solus de multis remansi prima frontis acie.

9. Ima vallis retrospexi, verticemque iuieri,
ubi suos inimicos rex fortis Hlotharius
expugnabat fugientes usque forum rivuli.

10. Karoli de parte vero, Hludovici pariter
albent campi vestimentis mortuorum lineis,
velut solent in autumno albescere avibus.

11. Laude pugna non est digna, nec canatur melode,
Oriens, meridianus, Occidens et Aquilo
plangant illos qui fuerunt illic casu mortui.

12. Maledicta dies illa, nec in anni circulo
numeretur, sed radatur ab omni memoria,
iubar solis illi desit, aurora crepusculo.

13. Noxque illa, nox amara, noxque dura nimium,
in qua fortes ceciderunt, proelio doctissimi,
pater, mater, soror, frater, quos amici fleverant.

14. O luctum atque lamentum! nudati sunt mortui,
horum carnes vultur, corvus, lupus vorant acriter:
orrent, carent sepulturis, vanum iacet cadaver.

15. Ploratum et ululatum nec describo amplius:
unusquisque quantum potest restringatque lacrimas,
pro illorum animabus deprecemur domin.

TRANSLATION

Grasslands there should feel no dew, showers, or good rain,
ground where great men, most skilled in battle, died,
men mourned by fathers, mothers, sisters, brothers, friends.

Here, the dreadful deeds, my poem's theme, were done,
and I, Angilbert, saw them; I fought with the others,
and I alone of all those in the front line, live on.

I looked back at the valley and the high hill
where valiant King Lothar saw his adversaries flee,
and forced them before him to the river's ford.

King Ludwig's men, or those of Charles? No matter which,
the fields are white with the shroud-like coats of the slain,
as linen blanched in autumn under a bird-filled sky.

Let no songs of praise be made for this struggle.
North, south, west, and east must bewail
the men who found death there on that day.

May that day be cursed, no longer counted
in the cycle of the turning year, but struck from memory;
may no sun shine on it, no dawn break into its darkness.

Night, too. That night of hard and bitter sorrow
in which the brave and battle-seasoned died,
mourned by father, mother, sister, brother, friends.

O grief and tears! The dead lie naked, stripped,
while vultures, wolves, and crows feed on their flesh
as they lie unburied, corpses, empty shells,

Past all lamenting. I can write no more.
Let men cope as they can with their own tears,
and let us all pray for the souls of the fallen.

www.ingramcontent.com/pod-product-compliance
Lightning Source LLC
LaVergne TN
LVHW091716070225
803225LV00002B/79